# Lobmeyr Contemporary

**Entwürfe seit 2000**

**Design since 2000**

Herausgegeben von  Edited by
J. & L. Lobmeyr
Leonid Rath, Andreas Rath, Johannes Rath

Birkhäuser

# Inhalt

# Content

Als sechste Generation eines fast 200 Jahre alten Traditionsunternehmens, dessen Produkte sich in Museen, Büchern und den wichtigsten Gebäuden der Welt befinden, haben wir uns von Anfang an die Frage gestellt, was denn dieses Unternehmen im Wesen ausmacht und welche Rolle es im Heute spielen kann. Was uns inspirierte, waren die Neugier und Offenheit unserer Vorgänger und das menschliche Bestreben, es einfach besser machen zu wollen. In einer Zeit, in der es scheinbar von allem mehr als genug gibt, in der andererseits immer mehr Menschen das Bedürfnis haben, sich mit weniger Produkten, jedoch in besserer Qualität, zu umgeben, sehen wir darin einen zukunftsfähigen Ansatz.

Das handwerkliche und ästhetische Wissen, das wir und unsere Mitarbeiter geerbt haben, für die Menschen von heute erfahrbar und genießbar zu machen, war seit unserer Übernahme also das deklarierte Ziel. Große Teile des Sortiments entsprachen bereits diesem Anspruch, wie Ludwig Lobmeyrs schlichtes Trinkservice No.4, Adolf Loos' Becherservice oder Haerdtls Kugeldose. Manche Produkte mussten nur leicht adaptiert werden, wie Hans Harald Raths Alpha-Service, das wir etwas zarter und in Farbe aufgelegt haben. Vieles war aber nicht mehr zeitgemäß und wurde ausgelistet. Es machte Platz für Neues – für Glas und Licht, das heutige Bedürfnisse trifft. Um dieses Heutige besser zu treffen, suchten wir die Kooperation mit externen Designern, die ja gute Beobachter sind. Monica Singer und später das Team der Vienna Design Week haben uns geholfen, die richtigen Kontakte zu knüpfen. Wir waren überrascht über das große Interesse und die Qualität der Auseinandersetzung mit den traditionellen Möglichkeiten und historischen Ursprüngen klassischer Produkte. Die alte Zeit schien weit genug weg, um neu entdeckt zu werden. Auch Kunden und Händler waren begeistert, und es entstand eine erfreuliche Dynamik.

Die wunderbaren Materialien Glas und Licht, ihr Wesen und ihre Kulturgeschichte immer wieder radikal zu hinterfragen. Archetypische Formen zu entdecken und möglichst gut umzusetzen. Handwerk im Produkt erfahrbar zu machen. Gegenstände für den Genuss zu schaffen, die nicht langweilig werden, sondern zu denen man eine Beziehung aufbaut. Das alles sind Gedanken, die unsere Arbeit motivieren.

Es ist tatsächlich unsere Überzeugung, dass gut gestaltete und ausgeführte Produkte einen positiven Einfluss auf den Nutzer haben. Gerade Essen und Trinken decken, ebenso wie Licht, so wesentliche Grundbedürfnisse ab und beeinflussen uns Menschen ganz unmittelbar. Hier gestaltend wirken zu können, ist eine große Verantwortung und gleichzeitig eine anhaltend spannende Herausforderung.

As the sixth generation of a family enterprise with a tradition stretching back almost 200 years and products that can be found in museums, books and the world's most significant buildings, we have often asked ourselves what it is that constitutes the essence of this company and what role it can play in today's world. The source of our inspiration has been the curiosity and openness of our predecessors and the simple human aspiration to improve on what has come before. In a time in which, on the one hand, there seems to be more than enough of everything and, on the other, more people want to surround themselves with less products but of a better quality, we see the potential for a sustainable approach to the development of our company.

Making the artisanal and aesthetic knowledge that we and our staff have inherited into something that can be experienced and enjoyed by people today has thus been a declared aim of our product development since we have taken over management of the firm. Large parts of the range of products dating back to previous generations already satisfied this criterion for us, such as Ludwig Lobmeyr's No.4 drinking set, Adolf Loos' tumbler set and Haerdtl's candy dish. Some products have had to be only slightly adapted, such as Hans Harald Rath's Alpha set, which we have issued in a more delicate version and colours. However, a large number of designs were no longer in keeping with the time and have been discontinued. This has opened up new scope – for glass and light that meets today's needs. In order to better realize this contemporary character, we have sought out collaborations with outside designers, who are of course good observers. Monica Singer and later the team from the Vienna Design Week helped us to make the right contacts, and we have been surprised by the high level of interest and the quality of engagement with the traditional possibilities and historical origins of classic products. The old times now seem far enough away to be rediscovered. Clients and dealers have also been very impressed and a highly gratifying dynamic has developed.

Continually and radically exploring the wonderful materials glass and light, their essence and cultural history, discovering archetypical forms and utilizing them as well as possible, making artisanship experience tangible in the product, creating pleasurable objects that do not get boring and to which people can build a relationship – these are all ideas that motivate our work.

It is our conviction that well designed and manufactured products have a positive influence on their users. Eating and drinking, like light, meet fundamental needs and directly influence us as people. Being able to shape

Produziert wird in Kleinserie, in Wien und dem näheren Umfeld, eine Grundvoraussetzung, um die Qualität zu halten. Es sind zu viele Details, die der Handwerker verstehen und täglich umsetzen muss, als dass man sie in einem Briefing zu weitab gelegenen Produzenten schicken könnte. So stehen wir jeden Tag selbst in der Werkstätte und sind bei der Wareneingangskontrolle dabei, um zu prüfen, ob die Idee der Designs in den Produkten zum Leben kommt.

Es macht uns auch besondere Freude, mit Designern zu arbeiten, die sich für unser Material und unsere Herangehensweise begeistern lassen. Einige neue Entwürfe sind von vornherein für den Verkauf und die Benutzung konzipiert, bei anderen überwiegt aber der experimentelle Charakter. Wir glauben, es ist wichtig, neugierig und offen zu bleiben – für Hersteller, Designer und Handwerker, aber wir sind auch froh, in einer Zeit zu leben, in der Kunden für diese konzeptuellen Entwürfe Interesse finden und uns ermöglichen, diesen Weg zu gehen. Nach über 100 neuen Lobmeyr-Designs ist es an der Zeit, ein Resümee über diese erste Etappe zu ziehen. Mit diesem Buch laden wir Sie ein, sich mit uns auf die Reise zu begeben und mit uns zu beurteilen, ob es uns gelungen ist, diese Welt schöner und vielleicht auch ein Stück besser zu machen.

Andreas, Leonid und Johannes Rath

the way these needs are satisfied is a great responsibility and at the same time an ongoing and exciting challenge. We manufacture our products in small series in Vienna and its immediate vicinity – a basic prerequisite for ensuring the maintenance of high quality. Sending briefings to manufacturers further afield is not possible due to the fact that there are simply too many details our artisans need to understand and implement on a daily basis. We ourselves are present in our firm's workshops every day and take part in the inspection of incoming products in order to check whether the idea behind a design has indeed come to life in the end product.

It is also a particular source of enjoyment for us to be able to work with designers who are inspired by our material and approach. Some new designs are quite consciously conceived for retail and use, while in the case of others the emphasis is on their experimental character. We believe that it is important for manufacturers, designers and artisans to remain curious and open. And we ourselves are also happy to be living in a time in which clients are finding interest in these conceptual designs and making it possible for us to pursue this path. After more than 100 new Lobmeyr designs, it is time now to take stock of this first stage. With this book we would like to invite you to join us on this journey and assess with us whether we have managed to make this world a more beautiful and perhaps also a slightly better place.

Andreas, Leonid and Johannes Rath

### Christoph Thun-Hohenstein
Generaldirektor, Österreichisches Museum für angewandte Kunst

*Das MAK und Lobmeyr verbindet eine lange Geschichte der Wertschätzung füreinander und vor allem eine gemeinsame Leidenschaft und Liebe für Glas: Es gibt kein Material, das Schönheit und Fragilität in so selbstverständlicher Anmut vereint. Das vorliegende Buch zeugt vom Mut eines Familienunternehmens, die zeitgenössische Auseinandersetzung mit Glas kreativ und nachhaltig voranzutreiben. Das neu erwachte Interesse an hochwertigem (Kunst-)Handwerk lässt für Lobmeyr eine glänzende Zukunft erwarten, in der wir uns noch auf zahlreiche magische Impulse in der weitgespannten Kunst des Glases freuen dürfen.*

### Lilli Hollein
Mitbegründerin und Direktorin der Vienna Design Week

*Andreas, Leonid und Johannes Rath haben etwas Besonderes erreicht und mit ihrem Interesse und ihrer Offenheit internationalen Köpfen aus Design, Architektur und Kunst die Türen zu ihren Werkstätten geöffnet. Die Vielfalt an technischem Wissen und handwerkerischen Möglichkeiten, die dieses Haus vereint, ist ein unerschöpflicher Fundus an Inspiration. Die bereits elf Kooperationen im Rahmen der* Passionswege *der Vienna Design Week haben immer wieder überraschende Resultate hervorgebracht.*

### Alice Rawsthorn
Designkritikerin und Autorin, London

*Lobmeyr verfügt über eine so reiche Geschichte in der Glasherstellung. Faszinierend, wie das Können, das Wissen und die Leidenschaft seiner Werkstätten auf die Werke ganz unterschiedlicher moderner Designer übertragen werden. Alle diese Gestalter interpretieren das Erbe und die Ressourcen von Lobmeyr auf sehr unterschiedliche Weise. Und zusammengenommen zeichnen diese Arbeiten ein fesselndes Porträt der zeitgenössischen Glasgestaltung.*

### formafantasma
Designer, Amsterdam

*Wir wollten schon immer für Lobmeyr arbeiten. Lobmeyr ist eines jener seltenen Unternehmen, das sich seiner Wurzeln bewusst ist. Sie respektieren handwerkliches Können, fürchten aber keine Veränderungen. Sie wissen, dass das Produzieren Verantwortung, aber auch Freude bringt. Sie wissen, dass ein Glas nur ein Glas, eine Vase nur eine Vase ist, dass aber die Art, wie ein Glas geblasen, wie ein kleines Detail graviert, wie ein Henkel angesetzt wird, ein Objekt von einem belanglosen Alltagsgegenstand zu etwas Einmaligem machen kann. Dieses Bewusstsein ist es, das die von Lobmeyr produzierten Objekte so besonders macht – sie erwecken das Gefühl von Liebe und Aufmerksamkeit.*

### Christoph Thun-Hohenstein
General Director, Austrian Museum of Applied Arts

*The MAK and Lobmeyr are linked by a long history of mutual esteem, and above all by a shared passion for – and love of – glass. There is no other material that unites beauty and fragility with such self-evident grace. This book testifies to the courage shown by a family company in its creative and sustainable promotion of the contemporary engagement with glass. The newly awakened interest in high-quality craftwork suggests that Lobmeyr has a bright future and that we can look forward to a multitude of magical impulses in the wide-ranging art of glass.*

### Lilli Hollein
Director and co-founder of Vienna Design Week

*Andreas, Leonid and Johannes Rath have achieved something remarkable and, with their interest and openness, have opened the doors of their studios to international figures from the spheres of design, architecture and art. The variety of technological and artisanal knowledge and possibilities that this company brings together is an inexhaustible source of inspiration, and the results of the eleven collaborations that have taken place so far within the framework of the* Vienna Design Week Passionswege *have all been strikingly distinct from one another.*

### Alice Rawsthorn
Design critic and author, London

*Lobmeyr has such a rich history in glassmaking that it has been fascinating to see the skill, knowledge and verve of its workshops being applied to the work of a diverse group of contemporary designers. Each of those designers has interpreted Lobmeyr's heritage and resources very differently. Collectively their work produces a compelling portrait of contemporary glass design.*

### formafantasma
Designers, Amsterdam

*We always wanted to work for Lobmeyr. Lobmeyr is one of those rare companies that is aware of its own roots. That has respect for craftsmanship but isn't afraid of change. That knows that producing is a responsibility but also a joy. That knows that a glass is just a glass, a vase is just a vase; but how you blow a piece, how you engrave a little detail, how you attach a handle, are the things that raise objects from the mundane to the unique. This awareness is what makes the objects produced by Lobmeyr so special: they evoke feelings of love and care.*

**Deyan Sudjic**
Direktor, Design Museum London

*Über sechs Generationen folgt Lobmeyr nicht nur den Entwicklungen im Design, sondern prägt diese auch mit. Seit Beginn bietet Lobmeyr Glas als das Rohmaterial an, an dem manche der bedeutendsten Architekten und Gestalter der jeweiligen Zeit ihre Talente erproben. Und auch am Beginn des 21. Jahrhunderts gelingt es Lobmeyr, die bedeutendsten Designer einer neuen Generation zu finden – nicht als Trophäen, sondern als das kreative Kraftzentrum seiner sich weiter fortsetzenden Entwicklung.*

**Tony Chambers**
Chefredakteur, Wallpaper* magazine, London

*Meine besondere Leidenschaft gehört den scheinbar weit auseinanderliegenden Disziplinen der Typografie und des Glasmachens. Typografisches Design ist das sichtbar gemachte Wort: die Kunst, das Handwerk und die Wissenschaft der klaren Kommunikation. Gutes Glasdesign hat natürlich auch mit Klarheit zu tun; im Idealfall repräsentiert es die perfekte Balance von Form und Funktion, von Ästhetik und Nützlichkeit. Und niemand macht bessere Gläser als Lobmeyr. Ich frage mich schon seit Langem, warum mich Lobmeyr in solche Bewunderung versetzt. Es ist nicht nur die Präzision, die Erlesenheit, die unglaubliche Feinheit der Produkte. Es sind wohl auch die Parallelen zu der von mir so geschätzten Typografie und die Klarheit, die in deren Erscheinung und Wesenszweck liegt.*

**Jean-Luc Olivié**
Chefkurator, Glasabteilung des Musée des Arts Décoratifs, Paris

*Es ist bewundernswert, wie diese ehrwürdige Luxusmarke mit Esprit, Respekt und Tatkraft ihr Erbe weiterträgt. Im Bewusstsein ihrer historischen, zu zeitlosen Klassikern gewordenen Produkte baut das Team mit Geduld, höchstem Anspruch und Präzision an einer Unternehmenslinie für das 21. Jahrhundert, jenseits einer ephemeren, rein medialen Produktwelt. So erneuert sich die Anmutung von Luxus in der Einfachheit und das Raffinement, das den Gläsern von Lobmeyr eigen ist.*

**Murray Moss**
Design entrepreneur, New York

*Neben der Einführung neuer Arbeiten verstanden die drei jungen Cousins die Veränderung der modernen Lebensweise bei ihren Altersgenossen. So müssen beispielsweise Wasser- und Weingläser auf der Tafel nicht mehr länger „eine Sprache sprechen", wie das früher die Regel war. Man wählt aus verschiedenen Mustern, sodass sich am Tisch eine „Konversation" zwischen den Designern entspinnt, genauso interessant wie (hoffentlich) die Unterhaltung der anwesenden Gäste.*

**Deyan Sudjic**
Director, Design Museum London

*Through six generations, Lobmeyr has not just traced but also helped to shape the evolution of the culture of design. Decade after decade Lobmeyr has offered glass as the raw material on which some of the greatest architects and designers of their times have exercised their talents. At the beginning of the 21st century it was still finding the most significant of a new generation of designers, not as trophies but as the creative core for its continuing evolution.*

**Tony Chambers**
Editor-In-Chief, Wallpaper* magazine, London

*My two enduring passions are for the seemingly disparate disciplines of typography and glassware. Typographic design is the word made visible. The art, craft, science of clear communication. Good glassware design is, of course, also about clarity and at best represents the perfect balance of form and function, of aesthetics and utility. And no one does better glassware than Lobmeyr. I've long wondered why I hold Lobmeyr in such awe. It's not only the precise, delicate and unfathomably fine nature of the product – it's perhaps the parallels with my beloved typography and the purity inherent in both their appearance and their objective.*

**Jean-Luc Olivié**
Chief curator, Glass Department, Musée des Arts Décoratifs, Paris

*I admire the heritage stewardship of this venerable luxury brand, cared for with esprit, respect, and dynamism. Conscientious and proud of its historical wares, now timeless classics, the Lobmeyr team is shaping the lines of the 21st century with patience, expertise, and precision, creating products that are a far cry from the ephemeral world of pure media hype. The feeling of luxury is being renewed through the simplicity and unique refinement of the superb Lobmeyr glassware.*

**Murray Moss**
Design entrepreneur, New York

*In addition to the introduction of new work, the three young cousins' understood the shift in modern living adapted by their peers, wherein for example the wine and water glasses no longer necessarily followed the old paradigm of speaking in one 'voice' at the table. The crystal now was chosen from a variety of patterns, allowing one to set their table with as interesting a 'conversation' between the various designers represented as that hopefully taking place between their various dinner guests.*

## Ein Garten aus Glas
Kirsty Bell

## A Garden of Glass
Kirsty Bell

„Seit mindestens zweitausend Jahren wird Glas herge-stellt", schreibt der Soziologe Richard Sennet in *Handwerk*, und verwendet diesen vielseitigen Werkstoff dazu, das Wesen von Perfektion und Eigenart zu demonstrieren. „Erst wenn wir verstehen, wie etwas auf perfekte Weise gemacht werden kann, vermögen wir die Alternative zu erkennen: ein Objekt, das etwas Besonderes an sich hat und Charak-ter besitzt", schreibt er. „Luftbläschen im Glas oder Uneben-heiten der Oberfläche kann man schätzen, Perfektion dagegen lässt keinen Raum für Experimente und Abwand-lungen."[1] Der 1823 gegründete und familiengeführte Glas-und Lusterhersteller Lobmeyr widmet sich eben diesem feinen Gleichgewicht: ein hohes Niveau an Perfektion, das dennoch den Charme und die Ausstrahlung des Handge-fertigten besitzt.

Lobmeyr kann seine lange Geschichte und andauernde Vitalität auf eine bedachte Kombination von Tradition und Innovation zurückführen. Historische, heute noch relevante Entwürfe werden gefertigt und gleichzeitig wird die Zu-sammenarbeit mit zeitgenössischen Designern fortgesetzt, um die Breite des Sortiments zu erweitern und seine Bedeutung zu erhalten. „Gute Produkte funktionieren nicht nur", stellt Leonid Rath fest, einer der drei Cousins, die seit den frühen 2000er-Jahren den Familienbetrieb leiten. „Sie stimmen Menschen positiv, sie haben etwas, das uns im Alltag wohlfühlen lässt ... Gute Designs besitzen emo-tionale Beständigkeit – es macht uns Freude, mit ihnen zu leben."[2] Diesen Luxus repräsentiert Lobmeyr: eine Art Luxus ohne Snobismus, der unprätentiöse, elegante Gegen-stände schafft, die eine empathische Erfahrung bieten können, die mit der Zeit nicht nachlässt, sondern zunimmt.

Während Leonid Rath sich um die Fertigung der Glas-waren und die internationalen Händler kümmert, führt sein Cousin Andreas das Stammhaus in der Kärntner Straße in der Wiener Innenstadt, das Lobmeyr 1895 bezog. Für Luster, die Werkstätten und den Projektvertrieb ist Johannes zuständig. Die Büros, Werkstätten, Archive und auch die Wohnungen der Familie, in denen die Raths seit 1970 leben, befinden sich in einem zwischen 1780 und 1866 erbauten Biedermeierensemble in einer Seitenstraße nahe dem Schloss Belvedere. Die Unternehmensarchive stecken voller Zeichnungen und Fotos, die bis in das frühe 19. Jahr-hundert zurückreichen und von den berühmtesten Desig-nern ihrer Zeit stammen, unter anderem von Theophil Hansen, Josef Hoffmann, Oswald Haerdtl oder Adolf Loos. Sie sind Zeugnisse eines Familienunternehmens, das heute in sechster Generation besteht und mit der Geschichte Wiens als Zentrum innovativen Designs eng verflochten ist. Den drei Cousins liegt vor allem daran, die doppelte Tradi-tion aus Respekt für Handwerk und Materialkenntnis und dem Verlangen fortzuführen, dieses Wissen mit den am

"Glassmaking has been practiced for at least two thou-sand years," writes sociologist Richard Sennett in *The Craftsman*, and goes on to use this versatile material to demonstrate the nature of perfection and character in craftsmanship. "Only by understanding how something might be done perfectly is it possible to sense this alter-native, an object possessing specificity and character," he writes. "The bubble or the uneven surface of a piece of glass can be prized, whereas the standard for perfection allows no room for either experiment or variation."[1] Lobmeyr, the Viennese family-run glass company founded in 1823, is dedicated to this fine balance: a level of per-fection that nevertheless possesses the charm and charac-ter of something hand-made.

Lobmeyr can ascribe its longevity and continued liveli-ness to a considered combination of tradition and innova-tion. As well as the ongoing production of certain historical designs that remain relevant today, they continue to ini-tiate collaborations with contemporary designers which extend the breadth and maintain the eminence of the company's range. "Good products don't just function," says Leonid Rath, one of three cousins who have been in charge of the family-run company since the early 2000s. "They make people more positive, they have something that provides comfort in daily situations ... Good designs pos-sess emotional durability and make us want to keep them around."[2] This is the luxury that Lobmeyr represents: a kind of luxury without snobbery, creating unpretentious and elegant objects that can provide an empathetic expe-rience, one that does not diminish but increases with time.

While Leonid Rath takes care of glassware and new commissions, his cousin Andreas runs the shop in central Vienna's Kärntner Straße – Lobmeyr's home since 1895 – and Johannes is responsible for "Luster" or chandeliers. The family's offices, workshops, archives as well as living quarters – home to the Rath family since 1970 – are loca-ted in a courtyard, built between 1780 and 1866, on a side street near Belvedere Park. The company's archives are full of drawings and photographs that date back to the early 19th century by the most revered designers of the times, from Theophil Hansen to Josef Hoffmann, Oswald Haerdtl and Adolf Loos among others. These are testament to a family business now in its sixth generation that is entwined with the history of Vienna itself as a vital center of design innovation. The twin tradition of respect for craftsmanship and knowledge about the material, and the desire to harness this with the most forward-thinking of contemporary designers, is what the cousins are most keen to continue. They often speak of the "Lobmeyr DNA", while "das sind nicht wir" – that's not us – is the standard response to concepts or ideas that don't quite fit. What

meisten vorausdenkenden, zeitgenössischen Designern neu einzusetzen. Sie sprechen häufig von der „Lobmeyr-DNA", während „Das sind nicht wir" ihre Standardreaktion auf Konzepte und Ideen ist, die nicht ganz entsprechen. Was sie *sind*, oder was *es* ist, wodurch etwas der Lobmeyr-DNA entspricht und zu einem Teil von ihr wird, ist nicht ganz leicht zu durchschauen: Es hat etwas mit Gebrauchswert, Form und Design zu tun, mit Geschichten, Handwerk und Geschmack. Anmut, Eleganz und Understatement spielen ebenfalls hinein, doch letzten Endes ist es die schwer fassbare Qualität des Zeitgemäßen und zugleich Zeitlosen, die ein Glasobjekt dauerhaft und relevant werden lässt.

Dem Unternehmensgründer Josef Lobmeyr, einem Glasermeister aus Oberösterreich, folgten nach dessen Tod im Jahre 1855 seine Söhne Josef und Ludwig. Ludwig Lobmeyr war ein prominentes Mitglied der Wiener Gesellschaft: Er war Abgeordneter des Herrenhauses, im Jahr 1864 einer der Mitbegründer des Museums für angewandte Kunst, Gastgeber von Herrenabenden, und führte das Unternehmen an die vorderste Front der architektonischen und gestalterischen Entwicklungen der „Ringstraßenzeit", die Wien in eine moderne Metropole verwandelte. Die Richtung, die Ludwig Lobmeyr vorgab, hatte viel mit seinem Verständnis für das Glasmacherhandwerk zu tun, das aus seiner engen Beziehung zu den Handwerkern in den Werkstätten ebenso wie der Zusammenarbeit mit Künstlern wie Hansen entsprang. In seiner Autobiografie beschreibt Ludwig, wie dieser kultivierte Umgang ihm ermöglichte, den Geschmack, die Eleganz und das Understatement zu entwickeln, die langsam in die Lobmeyr-DNA einflossen: „Es verbesserte sich allmählich mein Geschmack, dadurch wurden meine Erzeugnisse schöner, vornehmer, edler. [...] So, glaube ich, bin ich dahin gekommen, wo ich stehe; es hat nichts Außerordentliches mitgewirkt, es ist auch nichts Außerordentliches geworden, sondern nur Besseres, als eben sonst geboten wird."[3]

Der Standard, den Ludwig Lobmeyr in dieser höchst produktiven Zeit und in aller Bescheidenheit setzte, wurde zur Richtschnur, an der sich die folgenden Generationen orientieren. Ludwigs Neffe Stefan Rath übernahm 1902 die Geschäftsführung und nach anfänglichen Spielereien mit Jugendstil und Art Nouveau trat Josef Hoffman an ihn heran, um Arbeiten für die Werkbund-Ausstellung in Köln 1914 zu entwickeln. Das war für Rath ein Wendepunkt, der seine Pläne für das Unternehmen stark beeinflusste. Wie er später in seiner Autobiografie schrieb, handelte es sich weniger um die „Erhaltung der Tradition", sondern vielmehr darum, „an der Spitze" von Innovation und Design zu stehen.[4] Es war der Anfang einer dauerhaften Partnerschaft mit Hoffmann und anderen Künstlern der Wiener Werkstätte.

they are, or what makes something correspond to and become part of the Lobmeyr DNA, is harder to put your finger on: it has to do with usage, shape and design, with histories, craftsmanship and taste. Grace, elegance and understatement all play a role, but ultimately it is the elusive quality of being both timely and timeless that can turn a glass object into something lasting and essential.

The company's founder, Josef Lobmeyr, a glazier from Upper Austria, was succeeded upon his death in 1855 by his sons Josef and Ludwig. Ludwig Lobmeyr was a vital player in Viennese society: a member of parliament, co-founder in 1864 of the Museum for Applied Arts and host of a Gentlemen's Salon, he pushed the company to the forefront of developments in architecture and design. This was the start of the "Ringstraßenzeit", which saw the transformation of the city into a modern metropolis. The medieval city walls were demolished, old moats filled in, and a circle of elegant new buildings including museums, an opera house and university buildings were built. Many lots were sold to a newly rising class of financiers and industrialists: a new elite living behind a stately order of impressive facades; with the old city behind them, they looked out towards the future. While the direction Ludwig took the company had much to do with his understanding of the craft of glass making – due as much to his close involvement with the craftsmen in the company's workshops as with his collaboration with designers such as Hansen – his role as a society host was also significant. In his autobiography, Ludwig describes how these cultural exchanges enabled him to develop the taste, elegance and understatement that eventually began to flow into the Lobmeyr DNA: "It gradually improved my taste, through this my products became more beautiful, more distinguished, more elegant. [...] That, I believe, is how I got to where I am now; it did not add anything extraordinary, it didn't even become anything extraordinary, simply something better than whatever else was on offer."[3]

The standard set by Ludwig during this highly productive period became the bar to which subsequent generations held themselves to account. Ludwig's nephew Stefan Rath took over in 1902 and after an initially dabbling in Jugendstil and Art Nouveau, he was approached by Josef Hoffmann to develop works for the 1914 Werkbund Exhibition in Cologne. This marked a change of direction for Rath which had a profound impact on his intentions for the company. As he later wrote in his autobiography, these were not intended to "maintain tradition" but rather to "be at the forefront" of innovation and design.[4] It was the beginning of a lasting partnership with Hoffmann, along with other artists from the Wiener Werkstätte.

Hans Harald Rath trat die Nachfolge seines Vaters Stefan an und zeichnete 1966 für das Design der legendären Sputnik-Luster für die New York Metropolitan Opera verantwortlich, 1952 für das radikal reduzierte Becherservice „Alpha", das dem schnörkellosen Zeitgeist der Nachkriegszeit mit kleineren Haushalten und einer utilitaristischeren Ästhetik entsprach. 1968 übernahmen Harald, Peter und Stefan Rath das Ruder und widerstanden dem Druck, das Unternehmen zu vergrößern. Sie konzentrierten sich stattdessen darauf, die hohen Qualitätsstandards zu erhalten und Handelsware sowie Luster im Sortiment aufzuwerten. Sie gründeten eine experimentelle Glaswerkstatt, in der die Produktion sich stärker der bildenden Kunst annäherte, und begannen in den 1990er-Jahren die Zusammenarbeit mit Designern von der Universität für angewandte Kunst, zum Beispiel mit Matteo Thun. Die zarte, mundgeblasene Kristallschale des Wiener Studio LucyD, *Liquid Skin*, ist so organisch geformt, dass sie sich in die Handflächen schmiegt, aus denen man Wasser trinkt. Sie wurde in die ständige Designsammlung des MoMA aufgenommen.

Die Ansprüche waren daher hoch um das Jahr 2000, als Leonid, Andreas und Johannes Rath das Erbe ihrer Väter antraten. Die Designwelt in Wien durchlebte einen grundlegenden Wandel: Die Nachwirkungen der Ostöffnung 1989 brachte in Mitteleuropa eine Periode großer Veränderungen, von urbaner Entwicklung und Bevölkerungswachstum; in gewisser Weise war sie der Ringstraßenzeit des ausgehenden 19. Jahrhunderts ähnlich. Trotz seiner glanzvollen Geschichte hatte jedoch Design aus Wien in den vorhergehenden Jahrzehnten keine besondere Rolle gespielt. Jahrelang war internationales Industriedesign bevorzugt worden und die angewandte Kunst hatte an Boden verloren. Doch nun begann sich ein erneuertes Interesse am Handwerk bemerkbar zu machen. Es herrschte eine Aufbruchsstimmung unter jungen Gestaltern mit dem Willen, dem Design abermals Bedeutung zu verleihen, indem sie sich auf das Wesentliche besannen und die Dinge selbst in die Hand nahmen. 1998 wurde in Wien *Das Möbel* eröffnet, ein Café mit nutzbaren Exponaten, das von jungen Designern betrieben wurde, die dort unter dem Motto *benutzen, kaufen, besitzen* eigene Einrichtungsgegenstände und Designs vorstellten. Kurze Zeit später, im Jahre 2004, fand im MAK, dem Wiener Museum für angewandte Kunst, *Blickfang* statt, eine der ersten internationalen Designmessen. Schließlich folgte die *Vienna Design Week*, die 2006 von Tulga Beyerle, Lilli Hollein und Thomas Geisler gegründet wurde und deren wichtigstes Format *Passionswege* experimentellen Kollaborationen zwischen Herstellern und Designern gewidmet ist. Diese

Hans Harald Rath succeeded his father Stefan and was responsible for designing the infamous sputnik chandeliers for New York's Metropolitan Opera in 1966, as well as the radically pared-down, stem-less *Alpha* drinking set in 1952 that suited the no-frills mindset of the post-war era with its nuclear family unit and its adoption of more utilitarian aesthetics. In 1968, Harald, Peter and Stefan Rath took the helm and, while resisting pressure to expand the company, concentrated instead on maintaining their focus on high standards of quality and on completing the assortment with goods for resale and an intensified development of chandeliers. They founded an experimental glass studio that brought the production closer in line with fine art, and during the 1990s began working with designers from the university of applied arts such as Matteo Thun, or the Viennese Studio LucyD whose *Liquid Skin*, a delicate mouth-blown crystal bowl organically shaped to fit in the palm of the hand, is now in MoMA's permanent design collection.

The stakes were high, therefore in 2000 when Leonid, Andreas and Johannes Rath stepped in to succeed their fathers. At this time, the design world in Vienna and beyond was experiencing a tidal change. Given the repercussions of the post-1989 period in Europe, this was a time of great change, urban development and population increase; similar in some ways to the *Ringstraßenzeit* of the late 19th century. Despite its illustrious history, however, design had played no significant role in Vienna in recent decades. For years, international industrial design had been prioritized and the applied arts had lost their footing, but now a renewed interest in hand craftsmanship began to be felt. There was a move amongst young designers to make design relevant again by returning to the essentials and taking things into their own hands. In 1998, *Das Möbel* ('the furniture') opened in Vienna, a café and usable exhibition space run by young designers that featured their own furnishings and designs under the motto "benutzen, kaufen, besitzen": *use, buy, own.* Shortly after, in 2004, *Blickfang*, one of the first international design fairs, began at MAK, Vienna's Museum for Applied Arts. This was followed by the *Vienna Design Week*, founded in 2006 by Tulga Beyerle, Lilli Hollein and Thomas Geisler, with a core section named 'Passionswege' devoted to experimental collaborations between manufacturers and designers. These developments cultivated a fertile atmosphere within which Lobmeyr could reexamine its philosophy and direction, and encouraged the new owners to work closely with young and largely unknown designers of their own generation as well as artists from other disciplines. An early

Entwicklungen schufen eine fruchtbare Atmosphäre, in der Lobmeyr seine Philosophie und Richtung auf den Prüfstand stellen konnte, und ermutigten die neuen Besitzer dazu, eng mit jungen und zumeist noch unbekannten Designern ihrer eigenen Generation und mit Künstlern aus anderen Disziplinen zusammenzuarbeiten. Ein frühes Zeichen für diese neue Richtung war die Neuauflage des „Wiener Achtel" 2005 von Miki Martinek. Dieses kleine, unprätentiöse Wein- oder Bierglas wurde als Einsteigerglas gesehen. Es signalisierte eine neue Hinwendung zur lokalen Kultur und zum alltäglichen Gebrauch. Ein Statement gegen die Tradition, ein aufwendiges Gläserservice in allen möglichen Größen zu besitzen, in einer Vitrine wegzusperren und nur selten zu verwenden. Das Glas steht vielmehr für eine Art Alltagsluxus, der es erlaubt, einfache, aber erlesene Produkte in das tägliche Leben zu integrieren; eine Verfeinerung des Alltags, die in einfache Freuden und persönliche Rituale investiert.

Wie so oft brachte diese Verschiebung des Interesses auch Konfrontationen mit sich: Auf der einen Seite stand der Wunsch, die Stagnation durch einen Bottom-up-Ansatz und den Einbezug vernakulären Designs zu brechen, auf der anderen der eher traditionsorientierte Geschmack langjähriger Lobmeyr-Kunden. Die drei Cousins stellten sich diesem Konflikt und begannen damit, die bestehende Lobmeyr-Kollektion zu straffen und den Fokus auf die für die Marke wesentlichsten Produkte zu legen. Sie studierten die Archive und legten einige Schlüsseldesigns neu auf, etwa Josef Lobmeyrs Biedermeierbecher von 1846, seinen allerersten Entwurf; oder eine eindrucksvolle Vase von Josef Hoffmann, die 2003 anlässlich des hundertsten Gründungsjahres der Wiener Werkstätte in Produktion ging. Die Originalzeichnung von ca. 1930 war zuvor nie ausgeführt worden. Bereits 2004 hatten die jüngeren Raths begonnen, neue Designeinflüsse in das Unternehmen einzubringen, angefangen mit dem österreichischen Produktdesigner Sebastian Menschhorn, der *Lebensblumen* entwarf, eine mit eleganten, orientalischen Textilien entlehnten Blumendesigns bemalte Serie. Das war die erste von mehreren Kollaborationen über die folgenden Jahre, darunter auch das Corporate Design des Unternehmens in den Jahren 2006–2008. Im selben Jahr begann auch Monica Singer, eine weitere junge Absolventin der Angewandten, in Teilzeit im Unternehmen zu arbeiten. Ursprünglich war sie für Zeichnungen für Gravuren und das interne Grafikdesign verantwortlich, brachte sich jedoch mehr und mehr in die strategische Designentwicklung des Unternehmens ein, indem sie eigene Kontakte und ihr Wissen einfließen ließ, um den Fokus des Unternehmens von innen heraus zu schärfen. Im heißen Wiener Sommer 2004 bauten Rath und Singer im Geschäft in der Kärntner

sign of their chosen direction was the 2005 reissue of the *Wiener Achtel* designed in 1998 by Miki Martinek, Viennese designer and Interior Design Professor at the School of Applied Arts. This small, unpretentious glass used for wine or beer was seen as an 'Einsteiger' or beginner's glass. It signaled a renewed embrace of the vernacular or popular, and a move away from the custom of having an elaborate set of glasses in many sizes kept locked away in a sideboard and rarely used. Instead it proposed a kind of everyday luxury, where simple but fine products could be integrated into daily life; a refinement of the everyday, investing in simple pleasures and personal rituals.

As so often happens, this shift of interest also brought with it a confrontation: on the one hand a desire to change the stagnant situation by adopting a 'bottom up' approach through an embrace of vernacular design, and on the other the more traditionally-oriented tastes of long-term Lobmeyr clients. The three cousins tackled this conflict head on, and began by consolidating the existing Lobmeyr collection and streamlining the company's focus onto the products that were most significant and vital to the brand. They studied the archives and reissued some key designs such as the 2002 edition of Josef Lobmeyr's 1846 Biedermeier Becher, his first-ever design; or a striking vase by Josef Hoffmann produced in 2003 to mark the 100th anniversary of the Wiener Werkstätte, from an original drawing from around 1930 that had never been fabricated. By 2004, the younger Raths had begun to bring new design influences into the company, beginning with Austrian product designer Sebastian Menschhorn, who produced *Lebensblumen*, a set of glasses painted with elegant floral designs borrowed from oriental textiles. It was the first of what became several collaborations over the following years, including the corporate design of the company from 2006–2008. In the same year, Monica Singer, another recent graduate from the School for Applied Arts, began to work part-time in the company. Initially responsible for making drawings for engravings and for in-house graphic design, she became more and more involved in the company's strategic development, introducing her own contacts and knowledge about the design scene in order to sharpen the company's focus from within. In the hot Vienna summer of 2004, Rath and Singer set up a water bar in the shop on Kärntner Straße, from which passersby could drink from a whole range of Lobmeyr glasses: a casual, dynamic event which helped to clear out the fusty, old-fashioned image of the shop. This became a key year for Lobmeyr's newest phase: the first *Blickfang* Design Fair was held at MAK; in March they presented Menschhorn's *Lebensblumen* in a Hamam in Vienna, and the classic *Alpha* glasses were produced in a new series of delicate colors.

Straße eine Wasserbar auf, an der Passanten aus einem großen Sortiment von Lobmeyr-Gläsern trinken konnten: ein lockeres, dynamisches Event, das dazu beitrug, das angestaubte, ehrwürdige Image des Geschäfts aufzulockern. Dieses Jahr wurde für die jüngste Phase bei Lobmeyr zu einem Schlüsseljahr: Die erste *Blickfang*-Designmesse fand am MAK statt; im März wurden Menschhorns *Lebensblumen* in einem Hamam in Wien präsentiert, und die klassischen *Alpha*-Gläser wurden in einer neuen Auflage in zarten Farben produziert.

Wenn es um potenzielle neue Designer ging, bestand Leonid Raths Strategie darin, sie das bestehende Sortiment studieren zu lassen und sie aufzufordern, etwas vorzuschlagen, was sie selbst gerne benützen würden, aber darin nicht finden konnten. Solche Initialprojekte führten oft zu einer weiteren Zusammenarbeit. Bei Menschhorn beispielsweise ergab sich die Arbeit mit fein geschliffenen, aber unpolierten Oberflächen, für die er *Gletscher* entwickelte, eine Vase, deren glattes Inneres mit ihren rauen, eisbergartigen äußeren Oberflächen kontrastiert. Singer wurde dagegen eingeladen, eine persönliche Karaffe zu entwerfen. Das Ergebnis war *Josephine* (2006), eine Karaffe mit einem einzelnen dazugehörigen Glas, die persönlichen Gebrauch, Ritual und Vergnügen betont.

Im Lauf der folgenden zehn Jahre wurden weitere internationale Designer an Bord geholt, wodurch eine lange und bunte Liste von Kollaborationspartnern entstand. Einige Verbindungen wurden von den Raths initiiert, andere kamen jedoch über die *Vienna Design Week* zustande, besonders über ihr Format *Passionswege*, das dafür konzipiert war, talentierte österreichische und internationale Designer mit dem handwerklichen Wissen etablierter Wiener Handwerksbetriebe zusammenzubringen. Da die *Passionswege*-Projekte im Wesentlichen experimentell waren, luden die Raths die Designer gewöhnlich zunächst in die Werkstätten des Unternehmens in der Salesianergasse ein. Im dortigen Hof, in dem bis zu dreißig Handwerker beschäftigt sind, passieren alle Stadien des Produktionsprozesses bis auf das Glasblasen selbst, das in ausgewählten, spezialisierten Manufakturen stattfindet, einige davon in den böhmischen Glasregionen, wo Lobmeyr schon im 19. Jahrhundert produzieren ließ. Die Werkstätten in der Salesianergasse widmen sich Schliff und Polieren, Gravur, Metallarbeit und Lustermontage, wobei die jeweils verwendeten Techniken über Jahrzehnte, ja Jahrhunderte, angeeignet und entwickelt wurden. Leonid beschreibt Lobmeyrs Produktionsprozess als im Wesentlichen entwurfsbestimmt und nicht durch Werkzeuge, Methoden oder die Verfügbarkeit von Komponenten eingeschränkt. Vielmehr werden die Werkzeuge, Verfahren und Komponenten ständig den Bedürfnissen des Entwurfs

When it came to potential new designers, Leonid Rath's strategy was to have them study the existing range and make a proposal for something they felt was missing that they would like to use themselves. Such initial projects often led to further cooperation. Menschhorn for example worked with finely cut but not polished surfaces, for which he developed *Gletscher*, a vase whose smooth interior is countered by its rough, ice-berg-like outer surfaces. Singer, meanwhile, was invited to design a personal carafe, and created *Josephine* (2006), a carafe with a single matching glass to emphasize personal use, ritual and pleasure.

Throughout the course of the coming decade, more international designers were invited on board, resulting in a long and varied list of collaborators. Some connections were initiated by the Raths, but others came through the Vienna Design Week, in particular its *Passionswege* section, conceived to bring together the talents of Austrian and international designers with the know-how of established Viennese manufacturing businesses. Given that the *Passionswege* projects were essentially experimental in nature, the Raths usually began by inviting the designers into the company's workshops on Salesianergasse. In the courtyard here, where up to thirty craftsmen are employed, all stages of the production process take place save the glass blowing itself, which takes place in selected, specialized factories, some of them in the Bohemian glass-regions where Lobmeyr had done some manufacturing back in the 19th century. The workshops in Salesianergasse are variously dedicated to glass cutting and polishing, engraving, metalwork and chandelier assembly, while the kinds of technology employed are the result of techniques developed during the many decades of the company's existence. Leonid describes Lobmeyr's production processes as essentially design-driven and not confined by given tools, techniques or available components. Rather, the tools, processes and components are constantly adapted, developed and extended in accordance with the needs of the design in order to realize its fundamental concept and thereby extend the possibilities of glass as a medium. The resulting products are a true collaboration between the knowledge and experience of the company and the designer's innovation and ideas.

For an early *Passionswege* project in 2009, British designer Max Lamb explored the process of glass-making with a series of tumblers designed to demonstrate each of its stages. Firstly, the art of mouth-blowing glass, with its paradoxical striving for consistency in a process unique and imperfect by nature. Then, the cutting of the glass and the development of form through the addition of incremental geometrically cut facets on a cylindrical

gemäß adaptiert, entwickelt und erweitert, um das jeweilige Grundkonzept zu verwirklichen und so die Möglichkeiten von Glas als Medium zu erweitern. Die daraus entstehenden Produkte sind ein echtes Resultat des Zusammenfließens von Wissen und der Erfahrung des Unternehmens und der Innovation und dem Ideenreichtum des Designers.

Für ein frühes *Passionswege*-Projekt im Jahr 2009 erforschte der britische Designer Max Lamb den Prozess des Glasmachens mit Becherserien, deren Design die grundlegenden Arbeitsgänge sichtbar machen sollte. Zunächst die Kunst des Mundblasens von Glas mit ihrem paradoxen Streben nach Konsistenz in einem dem Wesen nach unwiederholbaren und imperfekten Verfahren. Dann der Schliff des Glases und die Entwicklung der Form durch das Schleifen einer steigenden Zahl von Facetten auf einer zylindrischen Becherform. Und schließlich das arbeitsintensive Gravurverfahren: Auf dem ersten Glas der Serie wurde ein einzelner Punkt eingraviert, doch die Punkte vermehrten sich von Glas zu Glas, bis das letzte Glas mit dem Maximum von 641 Punkten übersät war. „Je kunstvoller und zeitintensiver die Gravur, desto teurer ist das fertige Glas", stellt Lamb fest und verrät damit einen Teil der Ironie des Projekts, bei dem die Kosten in direkter Korrelation zur Menge der Dekoration stehen. Im Jahr 2016 verwendete der Italiener Martino Gamper bei seiner zweiten *Passionswege*-Kollaboration die gesamte Bandbreite an verfügbaren Techniken: Schleifen, Gravieren, Polieren, Sandstrahlen, Handbemalung, Vergolden und Lüstrieren, und schuf damit eine limitierte Edition von 54 Prototypen, um den klassischen Old-Fashioned-Whiskybecher zu modernisieren. „Alle neuen Entwicklungen sind tief in der Vergangenheit verwurzelt", sagt Gamper. 18 dieser Modelle wurden in das Sortiment aufgenommen, und damit wurde aus den ursprünglich experimentellen Prototypen ein kommerziell tragfähiges Produkt entwickelt.

Leonid Rath beschreibt Lobmeyrs Sortiment als Garten, der sorgfältig gepflegt werden muss, indem Produkte, die nicht mehr gedeihen, durch neue ersetzt werden – ein Gedanke, der in dem von Sebastian Menschhorn gestalteten, ausfaltbaren Poster mit grafischen Darstellungen des gesamten Sortiments veranschaulicht wird, das regelmäßig neu aufgelegt wird. Neue Produkte kommen entweder durch Neuauflagen älterer Entwürfe hinzu, die weiterhin relevant sind; durch experimentelle Forschungsprojekte; oder durch klassische Produktentwicklung, die entweder von der Funktion eines Gegenstands gesteuert ist (wie beim pragmatischen Trinkservice *Wiener gemischter Satz* aus 2008, das POLKA gestaltete); oder sie entstehen aus dem Wunsch, die intrinsischen Qualitäten des Handwerks

glass. And finally, the labor-intensive engraving process: on the first glass in the series a single point was engraved, but the points increased glass by glass until the last glass was completely covered with 641 points. "The more elaborate and time-honored the engraving, the more expensive the finished glass," says Lamb, revealing something of the irony of a project where expense is directly aligned with amount of decoration. Nevertheless, he sees his concept as "a communication tool to reveal the skill-level and value of traditional crystal engraving." In 2016, for his second *Passionswege* collaboration, Italian Martino Gamper adopted the whole gamut of available techniques: cutting, engraving, polishing, sand-blasting, hand-painting, gilding and luster painting, to create a limited edition of 54 prototypes to update the old-fashioned whisky tumbler. "All new creations are deeply rooted in the past," says Gamper. Of these, 18 models grouped into three series have gone into production, thus devising a commercially viable product from the initially experimental prototypes.

Leonid Rath describes Lobmeyr's range as a garden that has to be carefully tended, in which products which are no longer flourishing are replaced by new ones, as can be seen in the fold-out poster with graphic reproductions of drinking sets and related products, designed by Sebastian Menschhorn and reissued regularly. New products are added either through re-editions of older designs which continue to be relevant; experimental research projects; or classic product development, driven either by an object's function (such as the pragmatic drinking set, the 2008 'Wiener gemischter Satz' designed by Singer under the design name POLKA) or by the desire to highlight the intrinsic qualities of craftsmanship (such as Murray Moss's engravings of tiny insects on the sides of Lobmeyr's signature breath-thin 'muslin' glasses). American industrial designer turned jeweler Ted Muehling was one of the first international designers with whom Lobmeyr worked. The drinking set he designed in 2007, 'Balloon', whose gently curving convex or concave glasses convey the physical process of air blowing into the glass, meets his own description of his work as both "extremely simple and sensible" and yet "a bit extravagant and elegant."[5] For Muehling, who works from a studio-cum-store in New York's Tribeca – a Wunderkammer-like environment crammed full of fantastic objects – the appeal of working with a small company like Lobmeyr is the lack of regulations. For his *Balloon* series, he was able to work directly with the glass-blowers in the factory to finesse the wooden molds into which the glasses are blown until finally reaching the perfect form.

zu betonen (wie bei Murray Moss' Gravuren von winzigen Insekten auf den charakteristischen hauchdünnen „Musselin"-Gläsern von Lobmeyr). Ted Muehling, ein amerikanischer Industriedesigner, der zum Juwelier umgesattelt hatte, war einer der ersten internationalen Designer, mit denen Lobmeyr arbeitete. Das Trinkservice *Balloon*, das er 2007 entwarf, vermittelt mit seinen sanft gerundeten konvexen oder konkaven Formen Glas als luftgefüllte Blase. Muehling beschreibt seine Arbeit als „extrem einfach und vernünftig" und gleichzeitig doch „ein wenig extravagant und elegant".[5] Für ihn, der aus seinem Atelier Laden im New Yorker Stadtteil Tribeca heraus werkt – ein an eine Wunderkammer erinnerndes Ambiente voller fantastischer Gegenstände –, besteht der Reiz der Auseinandersetzung mit einem kleinen Unternehmen wie Lobmeyr im Fehlen von Beschränkungen.

Im Jahr 2010 wurde der deutsche Produktdesigner Mark Braun zu einer Zusammenarbeit für die *Passionswege* eingeladen, aus der in der Folge mehrere neue Produkte für Lobmeyr hervorgingen. Sein Ziel – so sagt er – ist es, „ein Konzept zu entwickeln, um eine Geschichte zu erzählen", und das mithilfe einer Arbeitsmethode, die im Wesentlichen „materialgesteuert" ist. Für *Passionswege* adaptierte Braun Ideen zum „Luxus der Zukunft", die Hans Magnus Enzensberger in einem Essay 1995 skizziert hatte[6], dass nämlich Zeit, Aufmerksamkeit, Platz und Ruhe in Zukunft Konsumgüter als höchste Formen des Luxus ersetzen werden. In seinem Projekt wollte Braun darauf hinweisen, dass Wasser einer der wertvollsten und rarsten Stoffe ist, und entwickelte eine Karaffe, auf deren Oberfläche die topografischen Formen unterschiedlicher österreichischer Gewässer graviert sind. Die erste Edition wurde jeweils mit dem Wasser dieser Orte gefüllt. Braun, ebenso wie viele Designer, mit denen ich gesprochen habe, beschreibt Leonid als „guten Sparringpartner" und spricht liebevoll über das Unternehmen, seine Handwerker, die Familie Rath und die Möglichkeiten, die sie als Kollaborationspartner bieten.

Von den vielen experimentellen Projekten und Entwicklungen, die Lobmeyr ermöglicht, führt nur eine Handvoll zu Produkten, die in das Sortiment aufgenommen werden. Einige kreuzen nahe am Feld der Kunstinstallation, sind aber trotzdem erfolgreiche Produkte, wie etwa *Ripple* (2013) des Designerduos poetic lab, eine Kollektion von leuchtenden Glasblasen, die formal an gewöhnliche Glühbirnen erinnern, aber durch ihre unebenen mundgeblasenen Formen und eine sanfte Rotation ein wunderbares Licht- und Schattenspiel erzeugen. Andere Projekte sind eher konzeptuell wie etwa die kunstvolle, von Sanduhren inspirierte Installation *Time Elapsed* (2011) von Philippe Malouin, die von der *Vienna Design Week* initiiert

In 2010, German product designer Mark Braun was invited to collaborate for the *Passionswege* and went on to design several new products for Lobmeyr. His aim, he says, is to "develop a concept to tell a story," through a working method that is essentially "material driven." For *Passionswege*, Braun adapted the ideas on "The Future of Luxury" outlined by Hans Magnus Enzensberger in his 1995 essay,[6] whereby time, attention, space and quiet replace consumer articles as the ultimate forms of luxury. In his project, Braun wanted to suggest that water itself is among the most valuable and rare of materials, and developed a carafe with the topographical forms of various Austrian bodies of water engraved on their surfaces, filling the first editions of each with water from that place. Braun, along with many of the other designers I talked to, describes Leonid as a "good sparring partner" and was affectionate about this company, its craftsmen, the Rath family and the potential they offer as collaborators.

Of the many experimental projects, designs and developments that Lobmeyr supports, only a handful have led to products that were added to Lobmeyr's line, however. Some veer close to the territory of the art installation but are nevertheless successful products, such as the design duo poetic lab's *Ripple* (2013), a collection of free-blown crystal lamps that are reminiscent in form of ordinary lightbulbs, but create wonderful play of light and shadow through their uneven mouth-blown shapes and gentle rotation. Other projects are more conceptual, such as the elaborate hourglass-inspired installation *Time Elapsed* (2011) by Philippe Malouin, initiated by Vienna Design week and exhibited at the Victoria & Albert and MAK: a one-off sculpture that demonstrates the philosophical properties of glass-making and the time involved in its hand-crafted processes. Even these more cerebral projects have fed into the company's creative background, however; expanding the possibilities of the material and its craftsmanship while refreshing their public image.

Further collaborations have taken place with notable artists, designers and architects; among them Michael Anastassiades, formafantasma, Maxim Velcovsky, Helmut Lang, Stefan Sagmeister, BCXSY, Marco Dessí, Peter Noever, Tomás Alonso, mischer'traxler, and Hubmann • Vass, while the most recent projects include SANAA, Sebastian Herkner for Wallpaper* Handmade and Ilse Crawford.

Ultimately, the Raths' dedication to their company is driven not only by history, tradition, craftsmanship and the desire for innovation, but also by a deeply rooted passion for glass itself. Towards the end of his life, their great-grandfather Stefan Rath reflected on his relationship to the material to which he had dedicated his working life:

und später im Victoria & Albert Museum und im MAK ausgestellt wurde: eine einzigartige Skulptur, die das Wesen der Glasproduktion und der Zeit, die in ihre handwerklichen Verfahren fließt, philosophisch veranschaulicht. Selbst diese eher intellektuellen Projekte stärken das kreative Potenzial des Unternehmens, sie erweitern die Möglichkeiten des Umgangs mit dem Material und seiner handwerklichen Verarbeitung und beleben die öffentliche Wahrnehmung von Lobmeyr.

Über die Jahre gab es zahlreiche weitere Kollaborationen mit namhaften Künstlern, Designern und Architekten wie Michael Anastassiades, formafantasma, Maxim Velcovsky, Helmut Lang, Stefan Sagmeister, BCXSY, Marco Dessí, Peter Noever, Tomás Alonso, mischer'traxler und Hubmann • Vass. Aktuell wird an Projekten mit SANAA, Sebastian Herkner für Wallpaper* Handmade oder Ilse Crawford gearbeitet.

Letztlich ist die Hingabe der Raths an ihr Unternehmen nicht nur von Geschichte, Tradition, Handwerkskunst und Innovationswunsch motiviert, sondern von einer tief verankerten Leidenschaft für das Material Glas. Gegen Ende seines Lebens dachte deren Urgroßvater Stefan Rath über seine Beziehung zu dem Material nach, dem er sein Arbeitsleben gewidmet hatte: „Im Laufe meiner nun schon über sechs Jahrzehnte währenden Berufstätigkeit gewann ich nach und nach immer mehr Verständnis für unser einzigartiges, herrliches Material. Man wird begreifen – und mir sicherlich verzeihen –, wenn ich es bedenkenlos in seinen ästhetischen Wirkungen höher einschätze als Gold und Silber und alle anderen Werkstoffe. [...] So oder so war das Glas oder der Kristall immer etwas Geheimnisvolles, Mystisches, nicht ganz von dieser Welt."[7]

"Over the sixty years of my career, I gained bit by bit ever more understanding of our singular, wonderful material. You will understand, and surely forgive me, when I unheedingly estimate its aesthetic effects as greater than those of gold and silver and all other materials. [...] Glass or crystal always had something secretive, mystical, not quite of this world."[7]

1 Richard Sennett, *Handwerk*. Aus dem Amerikanischen von Michael Bischoff. Berlin, 2007, S. 137, 143.
2 Leonid Rath bezieht sich hier auf ein Konzept, das Jonathan Chapman in seinem Buch *Emotional Durability. Objects, Experiences and Empathy*, London 2005 sowie in seinem Essay „Design for (Emotional) Durability" in *Design Issues*, Vol. 25, Nr. 4, Herbst 2009, S. 29–35 vorstellt.
3 Waltraud Neuwirth, *Schöner als Bergkristall: Ludwig Lobmeyr – Glaslegende.* Wien 1999, S. 346f.
4 Stefan Rath, *Lobmeyr. Vom Adel des Handwerks.* Wien 1962, S. 19.
5 William L. Hamilton, „In the Studio With: Ted Muehling. Minimalism Comes Naturally". *New York Times*, 12. August 2004.
6 Hans Magnus Enzensberger, „Luxus – woher, und wohin damit? Reminiszenzen an den Überfluß" (1995), in: ders.: *Zickzack. Aufsätze.*, Frankfurt a. M. 1997.
7 Stefan Rath, Lobmeyr. *Vom Adel des Handwerks.* Wien 1962, S. 36.

1 Richard Sennett, The Craftsman, New Haven, 2008, p. 104.
2 Leonid Rath is referring to the concept introduced by Jonathan Chapman in his book "Emotional Durability. Objects, Experiences and Empathy", London 2005, as well as in his essay "Design for (Emotional) Durability", in: "Design Issues", Volume 25, No. 4 Autumn 2009, p. 29–35.
3 Waltraud Neuwirth, Schöner als Bergkristall: Ludwig Lobmeyr – Glaslegende, Wien 1999, p. 346.
4 Stefan Rath, Lobmeyr, Vom Adel des Handwerks, Vienna 1962, p. 19.
5 William L. Hamilton, "In The Studio With: Ted Muehling. Minimalism Comes Naturally" New York Times, August 12, 2004.
6 Hans Magnus Enzensberger, "Luxus – woher, und wohin damit? Reminiszenzen an den Überfluß" (1995), in: id.: Zickzack. Aufsätze., Frankfurt a. M. 1997.
7 Stefan Rath, Lobmeyr, Vom Adel des Handwerks, Vienna 1962, p. 36.

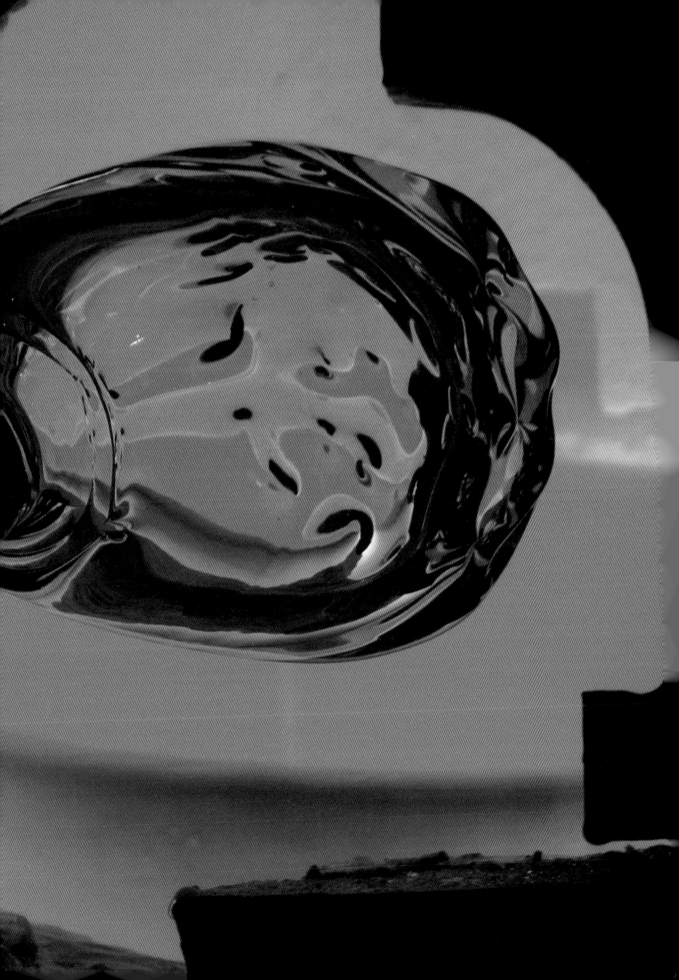

Josef Hoffmann

**Hoffmann Ringvase**  ca.1930 2003
Limitiertes Jahresobjekt (180 Stück)

Erstmals wurde eine ursprünglich nicht ausgeführte Originalzeichnung aus dem Lobmeyr-Firmenarchiv umgesetzt. Anlass war das 100. Gründungsjubiläum der Wiener Werkstätte. Die vierzig torusförmigen Ringe werden mit einem winzigen Schleifrad aus dem Kristall herausgeschält, von Hand seidenmatt poliert und mit einer kleinen Facette versehen.

**Hoffmann Ring Vase**
Limited edition (180 pieces)

This vessel represents the first realization of a previously unimplemented design based on an original drawing from the Lobmeyr company archives. The occasion for this undertaking was the 100th anniversary of the founding of the Wiener Werkstätte. The forty torus-shaped rings have been cut into the crystal with a tiny grinding wheel, hand-polished to a satin surface and ornamented with a small bevel.

**Trinkservice No. 267 – Alpha bunt** 1952 2004

    Die schönen, gespannten Formen dieses Becher-services liegen hervorragend in der Hand und eignen sich für jedes Getränk. Inspiriert von einem mittelalter-lichen Kupferbecher aus dem MAK, Wien, der seiner-seits von islamischen Formen beeinflusst war, sind die Trinkgläser im Sinne der 50er-Jahre stapelbar – „für den jungen Haushalt". Seither in kristallklarem Mousselin-glas gefertigt, wurden ausgewählte Formen 2004 in sechs zarten Farben, die fast nur im Mundrand sichtbar sind, wieder aufgelegt.

**Drinking set no. 267 – Alpha colors**

    The handsome, taut forms of this tumbler set fit snu-gly into the hand and are suitable for any type of drink. Inspired by a copper beaker from the Middle Ages on show at the MAK, Vienna, which was in turn influenced by Islamic forms, the drinking glasses are stackable in keeping with the desire for practicality in the 1950s – "for the young household". Since then the tumblers have been manufactured in crystal-clear muslin glass, and in 2004 selected forms were reissued in six delicate colors, which are almost only visible around the rim.

Sebastian Menschhorn

### Serie Gletscher 2005

Das enigmatische Glasobjekt macht die Schönheit der unpolierten Schliffflächen begreifbar, die Menschhorn als eine Metapher für Eis interpretiert. Ein geblasener Glaskörper wird so lange und so tief geschliffen, bis keine Rundung mehr übrig bleibt. Als Kontrast zum weichen, runden Hohlraum steht nun eine scharfkantige Außenform; sie beschützt die zarte Innenform und damit auch den Inhalt. Der bildhauerische Charakter wird durch die roh belassenen Schnittflächen bestärkt.

### Glacier series

This enigmatic glass object foregrounds the beauty of its unpolished cut surfaces, which Menschhorn interprets as a metaphor for ice. A blown glass body is cut until no curve remains. In contrast to the soft, round hollow interior, the exterior form becomes sharp-edged; it protects the delicate interior form and thus also its contents. The sculptural character is strengthened by the unpolished cuts.

Menschhorn hat den Prototyp mit dem Schleifer in der Werkstatt erarbeitet. 2005 wurde das Produkt zu einer Serie mit einer Kaviarschale, einem Teelicht, einem Schälchen und einer kleinen Vase erweitert.

Menschhorn created the prototype in his studio with a grinder. In 2005 the product was expanded into a series that includes a caviar dish, a tea light, a small bowl and a small vase.

Sebastian Menschhorn

### Serie Lebensblumen 2004

Das klassische Muster steht für Fruchtbarkeit und Lebenskraft und gleichzeitig für die geheimnisvolle und märchenhafte Geschichte der orientalischen Welt. Immer wieder taucht es in Menschhorns Arbeiten auf. Mit weißer oder schwarzer Emailfarbe von Hand auf den bunten oder klaren Glasgrund aufgemalt, entwickelt es die monochrome Zartheit von Spitze.

### Flowers of Life series

This classic pattern stands for fertility and vitality and at the same time for the mysterious and fantastical history of the Oriental world. It repeatedly emerges in Menschhorn's works. Hand-painted in white or black enamel on the colored or clear glass surface, it develops the monochromatic delicateness of lace.

Miki Martinek

### Wiener Achtel 1998 2005

Das Wiener Achtel – eine Neuinterpretation des klassischen Wiener Fasslbechers mit handgravierter Achtelliterfüllmarke – gewann 2007 den österreichischen „Adolf Loos"-Staatspreis für Design. Ein Glas mit Reminiszenz an das gemütliche Zusammensitzen beim Heurigen oder im Kaffeehaus steht heute für Understatement und die Pflege des kultivierten Gesprächs.

### Wiener Achtel

The Wiener Achtel – a new interpretation of the classic Viennese wine tumbler with a hand-engraved one-eighth-litre mark – was awarded Austria's "Adolf Loos" State Prize for Design. A glass evoking reminiscences of congenial get-togethers in the tavern or café, today it stands for understatement and the fostering of cultivated conversation.

POLKA

### Josephine 2006

Zusammen mit Monica Singer entstanden die ersten strategischen Ansätze in der Produktentwicklung seit 2000. Neben dem Begreifbarmachen von Handwerk stand Genuss und das Verwenden von Lobmeyr Glas im Alltag oder in persönlichen „Ritualen" im Fokus. „Josephine" verkörpert Lobmeyrische Formelemente – sie ist für den persönlichen Genuss bestimmt.

### Josephine

The collaboration with Monica Singer from POLKA gave rise to the first new strategic approaches to product development since 2000. The focus was on making artisanship comprehensible, pleasure and on the use of Lobmeyr glass both in the everyday context and in personal "rituals". Embodying formal Lobmeyr elements *Josephine* is designed for personal pleasure.

Sebastian Menschhorn

### Kugelmonogramm 2006

Das Monogramm als spürbares Ornament erst auf den zweiten Blick sichtbar zu machen, war das Ziel dieses Projektes. Die Idee war, personalisiertes Glas zu entwickeln, an dem man sich nicht sattsieht und das man gerne in die Hand nimmt.

### Pearl monogram

The goal of this project was to create a monogram as a palpable ornament that is only recognizable on a second view. The idea was to develop a personalized glass that one never tires of and feels good in the hand.

Oswald Haerdtl  Murray Moss

### Trinkservice No. 257 mit Insektengravur 1954 2006

Durch einen kleinen, aber präzisen Eingriff gelingt es, den Wert der feinen mundgeblasenen Becherform von Oswald Haerdtl zu erschließen. Sechs unterschiedliche Insekten werden in Kupferrad-Gravur, der Königsdisziplin der Glasveredelung, in die Glasoberfläche gearbeitet. Murray Moss, Designguru aus New York, war einer unserer wichtigsten Wegbegleiter beim Entdecken der eigenen Marke und bei deren Verbreitung.

### Drinking set no. 257 with insect engraving

A small but precise intervention suffices to develop the value of this fine, mouth-blown tumbler form by Oswald Haerdtl. Images of six different insects are worked into the surface of the glass using copper wheel engraving, the epitome of glass refinement. Design guru Murray Moss from New York was one of our most important consultants in the process of discovering and disseminating our own brand.

David Collins

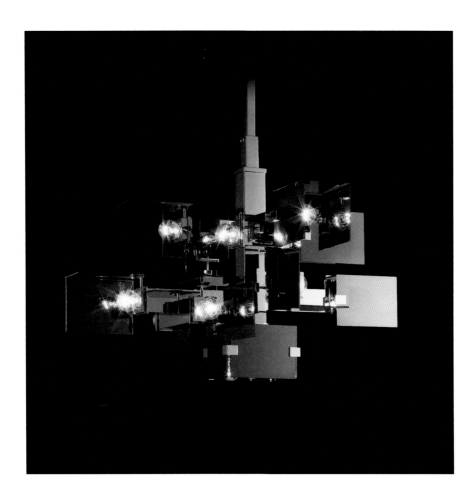

### David Collins Luster 2006

David Collins hat den Luster ursprünglich mit Lobmeyr für das Bob Bob Ricard Restaurant in London entwickelt, das sich am Stil der 1930er-Jahre orientiert. Heute wird er in verschiedenen Größen gebaut. Fein abgestimmte Oberflächen und Materialien und sorgfältig integrierte Technik machen die Qualität des Konzepts aus.

### David Collins Chandelier

David Collins originally developed the Luster with Lobmeyr for the Bob Bob Ricard Restaurant in London, the style of which is oriented to the 1930s. Today it is produced in different sizes. The concept is distinguished by subtly balanced surfaces and materials, and carefully integrated technology.

Ted Muehling

### Trinkservice No.279 – Balloon 2007

In Ted Muehlings erstem Projekt mit Lobmeyr werden Jahrhunderte historischer Entwicklungen reflektiert, um ein modernes Trinkservice zu entwickeln. Die Email-malereien und Gravuren von Schmetterlingen beziehen sich auf Zeichnungen der Künstler Maria Sibylla Merian und Jacob Hoefnagel aus dem 17. Jahrhundert; Fische und Augen sind beliebte Motive der Biedermeierzeit.

Ted Muehling's first project with Lobmeyr draws on centuries of historical trends to create a distinctively modern drinking set. Enamel paintings and engravings of butterflies reference the drawings by the seventeenth century artists Maria Sibylla Merian and Jacob Hoefnagel; and the fish and eyes stem from popular motifs of the Biedermeier period.

*Es bereitet mir mehr Freude, mich von der Vergangenheit
überraschen zu lassen, als die Zukunft erfinden zu wollen.*
　　　Ted Muehling

*I like the idea of being surprised by the past rather than
trying to invent the future.*
　　　Ted Muehling

Florian Ladstätter

**Orchideen Spiegel** 2007

Inspiriert von der spiegelsymmetrischen Form der
Orchideenblüten und deren enormer Formenvielfalt entwarf der Schmuckkünstler Florian Ladstätter diese Serie
von sechs spiegelnden Dekorelementen. Die Ausführung
in schwarzem Glas betont die exotische und fantasievolle
Anmutung der Orchideenblüten und nimmt die Funktion des „Spiegels" zurück. In bewusstem Kontrast dazu
gibt es die Serie auch in verspiegeltem Kristallglas.

**Orchid mirrors**

Jewelry artist Florian Ladstätter's designs for this
series of six decorative elements were inspired by the
mirror symmetry of the orchid flower and its enormous
variety of forms. The use of black glass underscores
the exotic and evocative character of the orchid flower
and attenuates the "mirror" function. A mirrored crystal
version of the series provides a deliberate contrast.

*Laisse du vieux Platon se froncer l'oeil austère;*
*Tu tires ton pardon de l'exès des baisers,*
*Reine du doux empire, aimable et noble terre,*
*Et des raffinements toujours inépuisés.*
*Laisse du vieux Platon se froncer l'oeil austére.*

Charles Baudelaire, „Lesbos" aus from
*Les Fleurs du mal*

Josef Lobmeyr

**Flakon No.8** ca.1830 2007

Limitiertes Jahresobjekt (184 Stück)

    Erstaunliches Biedermeier, Clown oder Weltraumflug-zeug? Der Parfumflakon war einer der ersten Lobmeyr-Entwürfe überhaupt und wurde auf der ersten Geschäfts-karte aus den 1830er-Jahren entdeckt. Viele Prototypen waren nötig, um die Zeichnung dreidimensional werden zu lassen und die aufwendig aus einem massiven Glas-rohling geschliffene Form zu erreichen.

**Flacon no.8**

Limited edition (184 pieces)

    Astounding Biedermeier, clown or spacecraft? This perfume flacon was one of the first ever Lobmeyr designs and was discovered on the firm's first business card from the 1830ies. Many prototypes were needed to render the drawing in three dimensions and to cut the elaborate form from a solid glass blank.

POLKA

### Trinkservice No.280 – Wiener gemischter Satz 2008

Das Wiener Designduo POLKA hat eine unkompli-
zierte Trinkglas-Serie für Lobmeyr entwickelt. Gläser,
die man oft und gerne verwendet – und dennoch strahlt
jedes Glas die Eleganz und Zartheit mundgeblasener
Lobmeyr-Gläser aus und hat seine ganz besondere
Geschichte: ob die önologisch korrekten Weingläser oder
die traditionelle Champagnerschale, die für über-
schwänglichen Genuss steht. Die Serie wurde mit den
„WienWein"-Winzern entwickelt.

### Drinking set no.280 – Wiener gemischter Satz

The Viennese design duo POLKA developed an un-
complicated series of drinking glasses for Lobmeyr. These
are glasses that one uses often and readily. Nevertheless
each one radiates the elegance and delicacy of mouth-
blown Lobmeyr glassware and has its own particular
history: whether one is dealing with the oenologically
correct wine glasses or the traditional champagne goblet
with its associations with exuberant enjoyment. The
series was developed with winemakers from *WienWein*.

Max Lamb

**blowing-cutting-engraving** 2009

„Passionswege" Vienna Design Week

Die Serie entstand als Installation im Rahmen der
Vienna Design Week 2009. Max Lamb beleuchtet die drei
wesentlichen Produktionsprozesse von Lobmeyr Glas.
„So wird jeder ‚geschlossene' Alpha-Becher absolut ein-
zigartig und zelebriert dadurch die Qualität der Hand-
arbeit von Lobmeyr-Glas", erklärt er zu „blowing".
„Engraving" spielt mit Wert und Menge von Ornament –
1 bis 644 Kugeln wurden live graviert. Aus „cutting" entwickelt sich später die „Quarz"-Serie.

**blowing-cutting-engraving**

*Passionswege* Vienna Design Week

The series was created as an installation for the
Vienna Design Week 2009. Max Lamb sheds light on the
three fundamental processes entailed in the production
of Lobmeyr glass. Explaining "blowing", he says, "Each
'capped' Alpha vase thus becomes totally unique and
in doing so celebrates the hand-made quality of Lobmeyr
crystal." "Engraving" plays with the value and quantity
of ornamentation – between 1 and 644 "orbs" were indivi-
dually engraved into the surface of the glass. "Cutting" led
to the development of the *Quarz* series.

**Quarz Serie** 2010                              **Quarz series**

Marco Dessí

### Trinkservice No. 281 – Grip  2009

Der Südtiroler Marco Dessí hat für Lobmeyr eine Serie aus Tumbler, Dekanter, Karaffe, Vase und Schale entwickelt, die Lust darauf machen soll, gerne und regelmäßig verwendet zu werden. Dessí zeigt, wie lebendig ein sehr reduzierter Entwurf durch handwerkliche Umsetzung werden kann. Der eigens entwickelte Lamellenschliff spielt mit technischer Ästhetik und vermittelt Funktionalität, denn bei der Konzeption war das haptische Vergnügen beim Trinken wichtig – der „Grip".

### Drinking set no. 281 – Grip

South Tyrolean Marco Dessí has developed a series for Lobmeyr comprising tumbler, decanter, carafe, vase and bowl designed to invite regular and pleasurable use. Dessí shows how skilled craftsmanship can bring a highly reduced design to life. The haptic pleasure of drinking played an important role in the conception of the design, in which a specially developed lamella cut projects a technical aesthetic and functionality – the *Grip*.

Die Zusammenarbeit mit Lobmeyr war sehr stark vom Dialog zwischen Werkstatt, den Raths und mir geprägt. Ein neues Produkt muss auch im Kontext der historisch bedeutsamen Kollektion funktionieren, aber auch eine zeitgenössische Position aufzeigen. Wir suchten genau nach der speziellen Aura, die ein Lobmeyr-Produkt umgeben muss. Durch Balance zwischen Reduktion und Schliff bei „Grip" haben wir zeitlose Objekte geschaffen.
  Marco Dessí

The collaboration with Lobmeyr has been very much shaped by the dialogue between the workshops, the Raths and myself. A new product has to function in the context of the historically significant collection, while also representing a contemporary aspect. We have been looking for precisely this aura, which a Lobmeyr piece needs to give of. In the case of Grip, finding a balance between reduction and cutting led to the creation of a timeless object.
  Marco Dessí

LOBMEYR

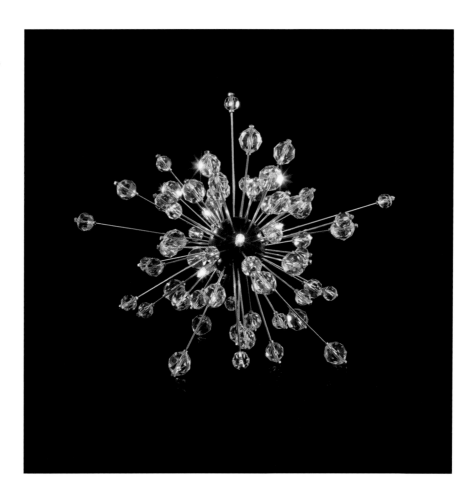

### Minisputnik 2009

1966 fertigte Lobmeyr die legendären Luster für die MET in New York. Inspiriert durch einen „Starburst" und Ausdruck der Aufbruchsstimmung der 1960er-Jahre. Seither werden die Luster in verschiedenen Größen und Ausführungen gebaut. Als die Luster 2008 zur Renovierung in Wien Pause machten, entstand die Idee, die größten „Sputnik"-Elemente als selbstständige Lichtobjekte zu bauen. Für zu Hause oder im Geschäftsbereich, zum Legen oder Hängen.

### Mini Sputnik

In 1966 Lobmeyr produced the legendary chandelier for the MET in New York. It was inspired by a "starburst" and expressed the mood of upheaval in the 1960s. Since then the chandelier has been constructed in different sizes and versions. When the chandeliers were being renovated in Vienna in 2008, the idea took shape to construct the largest *Sputnik* elements as independent lighting objects − for the home or business, for laying or hanging.

LOBMEYR

**Trinkservice No.267 – Tulipmania** 2009

    Um 1600 wurden Tulpen zuerst in Holland zum Spekulationsobjekt. Als die Preise für eine Tulpenzwiebel umgerechnet zwei bis drei Millionen Euro/Dollar erreichten, musste eine Regierung erstmals regulierend in die Wirtschaft eingreifen. 66 verschiedene Tulpen nach einem Versteigerungskatalog von Pieter Cos (1634) werden von Hand mit leuchtenden Emailfarben auf den klassischen Lobmeyr „Alpha"-Becher gemalt.

**Drinking set no.267 – Tulipmania**

    Around 1600, tulips became a speculative object in Holland. The rocketing of prices for a tulip bulb to the equivalent of two to three million euros/dollars resulted in a government intervening to regulate a national economy for the first time. 66 images of different tulips taken from an auction catalogue by Pieter Cos (1634) were hand-painted in luminous enamels on the classic Lobmeyr *Alpha* tumbler.

Mark Braun

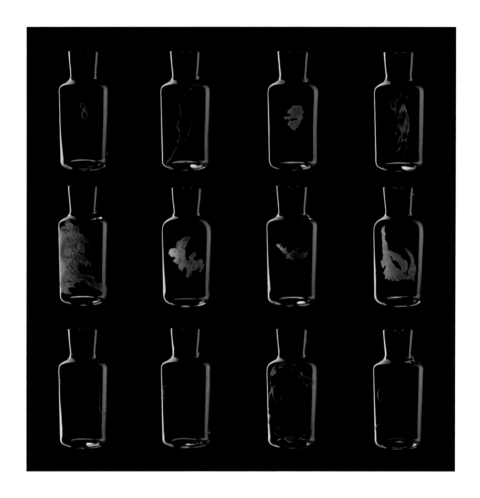

### Trinkservice No. 283 – Reichtum 2010
„Passionswege" Vienna Design Week

Reines Trinkwasser, als Metapher für den Reichtum
essenziellen, puren Designs in bester Qualität. 21 Karaf-
fen mit eingravierten österreichischen Gewässern wurden
zu den „Passionswegen" der Vienna Design Week 2010
präsentiert. Die erfolgreiche Installation wird weltweit
in Ausstellungen und Galerien gezeigt. Eine internationale Serie (2011), die Erweiterung zum Trinkservice und
verschiedene Dekore (2011, 2012 und 2017) folgten.

### Drinking set no. 283 – Fortune
*Passionswege* Vienna Design Week

Pure drinking water as a metaphor for the fortune
of essential, pure design of the highest quality. 21 carafes
engraved with images of Austrian lakes, glaciers and
rivers were presented as part of the *Passionswege* at the
Vienna Design Week 2010. The celebrated installation
was shown around the world in exhibitions and galleries.
It has been followed by an international series (2011),
an expanded drinking set and different or-namentations
(2011, 2012 und 2017).

Fortune und die Zusammenarbeit mit J. & L. Lobmeyr war und ist für mich ein wichtiger Schritt in meiner Arbeit als Gestalter. Produktqualität, Konzeption und Marke haben in dieser Kollaboration perfekt zusammengefunden. Es ist beeindruckend, mit welch feinem Gespür Leonid Rath und seine Cousins die Marke Lobmeyr führen und Zeitgeist mit Tradition wie selbstverständlich in ihrer Kollektion vereinen.

Mark Braun

Fortune and the collaboration with J. & L. Lobmeyr represent an important step for me in my work as a designer. This collaboration represented a perfect fusion of product-quality, conception and brand. It is impressive how sensitively Leonid Rath and his cousins manage the Lobmeyr brand, uniting zeitgeist and tradition in their collection in a way that seems so natural.

Mark Braun

Sebastian Menschhorn

### Serie Thom 2010

Wie gedrechselt wirken die mundgeblasenen, hand-
geschliffenen und handpolierten Glasobjekte. Thom be-
deutet in der Sprache der Khmer „großartig". Die Wurzeln
dieser Serie liegen in beiden Kulturkreisen – Europa
und Asien. Die Tempel von Angkor haben Fenstergitter
mit ähnlich gedrechselten Steinsäulen, aber auch in der
Architektur Josef Hoffmanns finden sich häufig entspre-
chende Profilierungen.

### Thom series

The mouth-blown, hand-cut and polished glass
objects look like they have been turned on a lathe. In the
Khmer language thom means "great". The roots of this
series are found in both cultural spheres – Europe and
Asia. The temples at Angkor have window gratings comprising similarly turned stone pillars. And the architecture of Josef Hoffmann, for instance, also often features
comparable grooved structures.

Ted Muehling

**Trinkservice No. 282**  2010

Die perfekt ausgewogenen Becherformen kommen
durch die zarte Ausführung und den flach geschliffenen
Boden besonders zur Geltung. Eine Herausforderung
für den Schleifer stellt der zum Anfassen einladende
Diamantschliff dar. Ted Muehling setzt mit diesem sensi-
bel-maskulinen Entwurf einen Kontrapunkt zu seiner
ersten Serie für Lobmeyr. 2015 wird die Serie durch
Vasen ergänzt.

**Drinking service no. 282**

The perfectly balanced tumbler forms are accentua-
ted by their delicate execution and flat-cut base. A particular challenge for the cutter is presented by the diamond
cut that invites one to touch to glass. With this design
Ted Muehling establishes a sensitively masculine counter-
point to his first series for Lobmeyr. In 2015 the series
was expanded to include vases.

Marco Dessí

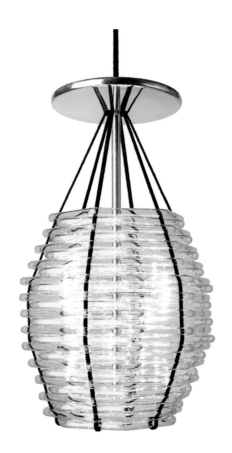

**Basket Luster** 2010

Barocke Glasarmluster waren um 1720 die ersten Kristallluster. Marco Dessí interpretiert in seinem Entwurf den Typus der Laterne neu. Dazu verflicht er hexagonal gebogene Glasrohre mit geflochtenen Seidenkordeln, einem weiteren klassischen Lusterelement. Obwohl das Prinzip ganz neuartig ist, strahlen die Luster im Glamour ihrer Vorbilder. Später wurden kleinere Versionen, Tisch- und Stehlampen entwickelt.

**Basket chandelier**

Baroque glass-arm-chandeliers emerged around 1720 as the first crystal chandeliers. In his design Marco Dessí reinterprets this lantern type by interweaving hexagonally bent glass tubes with silk chords, another classic chandelier element. Although the principle is completely new, the chandeliers exude all the glamour of their forerunners. Smaller versions as well as table and floor lamps have subsequently been developed using the same principle.

Sagmeister & Walsh

**Trinkservice No. 248 – Sagmeister on Loos**  2011/13

In seinem letzten Brief an Lobmeyr schlug Adolf Loos 1931 Alternativen für den Bodenschliff seines Services vor. „Schmetterlinge, Fliege, menschliche nackte Figur, kleine Tiere usw." wünschte der Purist in den Boden graviert. Zum 80-jährigen Bestehen der klassischen Bar-Serie beauftragte Lobmeyr Stefan Sagmeister, diese Idee weiterzuentwickeln. Die sieben Tugenden und die sieben Todsünden sind handgemalt und mit einer schwarzen bzw. weißen Emailschicht überzogen.

**Drinking service no. 248 – Sagmeister on Loos**

In 1931, in his last letter to Lobmeyr, Adolf Loos suggested alternative designs for the bases of his drinking set. The purist wanted engravings of "butterflies, flies the naked human figure, small animals etc." To mark the eightieth anniversary of creation of the classic bar series, Lobmeyr commissioned Stefan Sagmeister to further develop this idea. Images referencing the Seven Heavenly Virtues and the Seven Deadly Sins are hand-painted and covered with a black or white enamel coating.

Tino Valentinitsch

### Wiener Stutzen 2011

Der „Wiener Stutzen" verbindet die Form des griff-losen Stutzen mit der alten Technik, Glas „optisch" zu blasen. Valentinitsch reagiert damit auf die Renaissance des Wiener Gasthauses. 2013 durch das „Wiener Seiterl" (0,3 Liter) ergänzt.

### Wiener Stutzen

The *Wiener Stutzen* combines the form of the handle-free beer glass with the old technique of blowing glass "optically". Here Valentinitsch reacts to the renaissance of the Viennese tavern. In 2013 the series was expanded to include the *Wiener Seiterl* (0.3 liters).

MAK ART SOCIETY

### MARS Collection 2012

In Zusammenarbeit mit der MAK ART SOCIETY entstand zwischen 2006 und 2012 eine Serie von künstlerischen Interventionen auf Adolf Loos' Wasserbecher für Lobmeyr. 13 Becher – eine Kunstsammlung im Trinkformat. Heimo Zobernig, Manfred Wakolbinger, Eva Schlegel, Markus Schinwald, Georg Salner, Arnulf Rainer, Peter Noever, Helmut Lang, Brigitte Kowanz, Jenny Holzer, Franz Graf, Gregor Eichinger, Gunter Damisch.

### MARS Collection

Between 2006 and 2012, in collaboration with the MAK ART SOCIETY, a series of artistic interventions in Adolf Loos' water tumbler for Lobmeyr took place. The result was 13 tumblers – a drinking-art collection. Heimo Zobernig, Manfred Wakolbinger, Eva Schlegel, Markus Schinwald, Georg Salner, Arnulf Rainer, Peter Noever, Helmut Lang, Brigitte Kowanz, Jenny Holzer, Franz Graf, Gregor Eichinger, Gunter Damisch.

Adolf Loos  Hubmann · Vass

**Loos Champagner Kühler** 1931 2012

Die Architekten Erich Hubmann und Andreas Vass wurden beauftragt, den Entstehungsprozess der Serie, die Adolf Loos für Lobmeyr 1931 entwickelt hat, zu erforschen und zu dokumentieren. Eine kleine Loos-Skizze auf der Rückseite einer Visitkarte, die oft mit dem Service in Verbindung gebracht wurde, hat sie dabei besonders fasziniert. Die Architekten haben diesen Entwurf als eigenständige Serie für einen Wodka- bzw. Champagner-Cooler mit sechs Gläsern identifiziert

**Loos champagne cooler**

Architects Erich Hubmann and Andreas Vass were commissioned to research and document the design process behind the series Adolf Loos created for Lobmeyr in 1931. Hubmann and Vass were particularly fascinated by a tiny sketch by Loos on the back of a business card that has often been linked with the set. The architects identified this design as an independent series comprising a vodka or champagne cooler with six glasses and reconstructed the cooler in glass. The solid, hand-cut

und den Behälter als Glasobjekt rekonstruiert. Das massive handgeschliffene Objekt überrascht mit eindrucksvollen optischen Effekten. Weiters wurde ein Becher für „Feingspritzten" – Loos' Lieblingsgetränk – auf Basis des Erstentwurfs des Trinkservices entwickelt und der von Loos autorisierte Krug des Services neu aufgelegt.

object surprises with impressive optical effects. A tumbler for "Feingspritzter" – a mix of soda and champagne that was Loos' favorite drink – was also developed based on the initial design for the drinking set, and the accompanying Loos-authorized pitcher was reissued.

Michael Anastassiades

**Captured** 2012

Licht bricht sich im Kristall. Das natürliche Spiel dieser beiden Elemente in ein faszinierendes Objekt einzufangen war das Ziel dieser Kooperation. Eine für Michael Anastassiades typisch minimale, elegante und starke Metallstruktur gibt den feinen Glasteilen Position und Halt. Die in unterschiedlichen Varianten geschliffene Kristallkugel umschließt die Lichtquelle und bricht das Licht. Zwei Halbkugeln unterschiedlicher Größe umgeben den leuchtenden Kristall wie Sphären oder Orbits.

Light refracts in crystal. Capturing the natural interplay of these two elements in a fascinating object was the aim of this collaboration. The fine glass components are positioned and supported by a strong and elegant structure exhibiting a minimal character typical of Michael Anastassiades. Crystal globes cut in different variants enclose the light source and refract the light. Two half-spheres of different sizes surround the glowing crystal like orbs or orbits.

Licht, Schatten, das Spiel mit Geometrie und Raum machen den Reiz der Objekte aus. Der Lichtkörper wird als Hängeleuchte, Bodenstehlampe und Tischleuchte hergestellt.

*Ich bin seit jeher von Licht fasziniert, wohl weil ich versuche, all diese magischen Phänomene nachzuahmen, die sich in der Natur um das Licht ranken.*
　Michael Anastassiades

Light, shadow and the play of geometry and space lend these objects their particular appeal. The lights are produced as pendant lights, floor lamps and table lamps.

*I have always been fascinated with light probably as an attempt to imitate all these magical phenomena that occur around light in nature.*
　Michael Anastassiades

KIM+HEEP

### Lily Mokka 2013

Im Orient hat Glas für den Genuss von Tee und Kaffee eine lange Tradition. KIM+HEEP haben in Tests eindrucksvoll bewiesen, dass dünnes Lobmeyr Glas extrem temperaturbeständig ist. Das Designteam hat eine ausgewogene und funktionale Form geschaffen, die sich gut in Josef Hoffmanns „Patrician"-Service von 1917 einfügt. 2012 wurde die Teetasse und 2013 die Espressotasse mit vergoldeter Messinguntertasse entwickelt. Die gläsernen Tassen offenbaren die Farbe des Getränks.

### Lily Mokka

In the Orient the use of glass for the enjoyment of tea and coffee has a long tradition. In tests KIM+HEEP have proved that thin Lobmeyr glass is extremely temperature-resistant. The design team has created a balanced and functional form that fits well into Josef Hoffmann's *Patrician* set from 1917. In 2012 the teacup and in 2013 the espresso cup with gilded brass saucers were developed. The glass cups reveal the color of the beverage they contain.

Sebastian Menschhorn

### Serie Eckhart  2013

Aus rund mach eckig. Die zylindrische Form wird mit sechs Facetten geschliffen und poliert. Nur an einer Stelle bleibt das runde Rohglas erhalten. Dabei entstehen die grundlegenden Gegensätze von eckig und rund, roh und verfeinert. Es ist eine schwere, archaische Serie. Sie hat praktische Funktionen, kann aber auch unverwendet als Skulptur existieren. „Eckhart" ist die Schwester zu „Thom" und der noch nicht realisierten Diamantserie.

### Eckhart series

Take round and make it square. The cylindrical form is cut with six facets and polished. Only at a single point is the rounded raw glass retained. This gives rise to fundamental contrasts between angled and round, raw and refined. The series is heavy and archaic. It has practical functions but can also be left unused as a sculpture. *Eckhart* is the sister to *Thom* and the planned Diamond series.

poetic lab

### Ripple Light 2013

„Ripple" ist bewegtes Licht, das die Schönheit des Materials Glas ausdrückt und den Prozess des Machens zelebriert. Es besteht jeweils aus einem sich langsam drehenden „projection dome" und einem kleineren „lighting dome". Der gerichtete Lichtstrahl bricht sich in den sich bewegenden Wänden der großen Blase. Durch die unterschiedlichen Wandstärken ergibt sich ein faszinierendes Licht- und Schattenspiel.

### Ripple light

*Ripple* is light in motion that expresses the beauty of glass as a material and celebrates the process of creation. It comprises a slowly revolving "projection dome" and a smaller "lighting dome". The directed light beam refracts in the moving walls of the large dome. The different wall thicknesses produce a fascinating play of light and shadow.

*Während der Handwerker die Schönheit des Glases mit ge-taner Arbeit einfriert, bringt die elegante und präzise Rota-tion den Fluss des Materials zurück, so als wäre die Existenz der Glasblase ungewiss.*
　　poetic lab

*Whereas the work of the craftsman freezes the beauty of the glass, the elegant and precise rotation retrieves the flow of the material, lending an ambiguity to the existence of the glass bubble.*
　　poetic lab

formafantasma

### Trinkservice No. 284 – Alphabet 2013

„Alphabet" spielt mit der Vielfalt und bietet eine neue Variante des Tischdeckens an. Es gibt je sechs zartere Wein- und stärkere Wasserbecher und eine Karaffe mit Deckel. Die gravierten Dekore sind Zitate aus der Lobmeyr-Kollektion oder von dieser inspiriert. Der Wasserbecher wird über den kleineren Weinbecher gestülpt und dadurch ergibt sich das komplette Muster. Es entstehen so kleine „Wunderwelten" mit interessanten dreidimensionalen Effekten.

### Drinking service no. 284 – Alphabet

*Alphabet* plays with the idea of diversity and offers a new form of table arrangement. The collection comprises six delicate wine glasses, six sturdier water tumblers and a decanter with a top. The engraved ornamentation cites elements of the Lobmeyr collection or has been inspired by them. The water glass is placed upside down over the wine glass, thereby achieving the complete pattern. This gives rise to tiny "magic worlds" with interesting three-dimensional effects.

Mark Braun / Christoph Keller

**Schnapsglas Stählemühle** 2013

    Der Designer Mark Braun und der Meisterbrenner
Christoph Keller entwickelten gemeinsam ein neuartiges
Obstbrandglas – ohne Stiel, einem Destillierkolben nach-
empfunden. Die Hand umfasst den Korpus und erwärmt
den Obstbrand auf die ideale Temperatur. Der einge-
stochene Boden ist eine Reminiszenz an mittelalterliche
Becher.

**Stählemühle schnapps glass**

    Together, designer Mark Braun and master distiller
Christoph Keller have developed a novel glass for fruit
brandies – without a stem and inspired by the form of a
distillation flask. The glass body is held in the hand,
which warns the schnapps to the ideal temperature. The
recessed base is a reference to medieval beakers.

formafantasma

### Serie STILL 2014

Die Vorgabe von Lobmeyr an die Designer war ein mit Kupferradgravur veredeltes wertvolles Objekt. formafantasma machten daraus nicht ein Einzelstück, sondern eine Gruppe oder vielmehr ein Ritual, das uns daran erinnert, Wasser als die wichtigste Ressource unserer Erde, aber auch das Handwerk zu schätzen und zu genießen. Aus dem großen Gefäß wird mit einem Kupferschöpfer rohes Wasser in den mit aktivierter Kohle gefüllten Filter geschöpft. Das Wasser tropft, gereinigt,

### STILL series

The task given to the designers by Lobmeyr was to create a valuable object refined with copper wheel engraving. formafantasma responded by creating not a single piece but a group or rather a ritual that reminds us that water is our planet's most valuable resource while also prompting us to appreciate and enjoy the craftsmanship involved. A copper ladle is used to transfer unfiltered water from the large vessel into a filter filled with activated charcoal. The water drops, purified,

in das kostbar mit Wasserbakterien oder Haeckelschen Sporen und Pilzen gravierte mittlere Gefäß. Daraus wiederum kann dann Wasser in Gläser und Kupferbecher geschöpft werden. Die Kugeldose mit dem Löffel ist das Vorratsgefäß für die Kohle.

into the middle-sized vessel, which is sumptuously engraved with images of water bacteria or spores and fungi recalling the drawings by German naturalist Ernst Haeckel. The water can then in turn be ladled into glasses and copper cups. The bowl with the spoon holds the charcoal prior to use.

Oswald Haerdtl

### Kugeldose G und flach  1925 2015

Die Kugeldosen von Oswald Haerdtl zählen zu den bekanntesten Klassikern von Lobmeyr und verkörpern den Geist des Unternehmens wie kaum ein anderer Entwurf. Die Objekte mit der Kugel als archetypische Form, die für das Vollkommene steht, werden durch feine Details in Entwurf und Umsetzung zum unwiderstehlichen Must-have. 2015 wurden die große, fragile Globe und die flache, zierliche Variante sowie eine gold-lüstrierte Variante der Serie wiederaufgelegt.

### G and Flat candy dishes

The candy dishes by Oswald Haerdtl number among the most well-known Lobmeyr classics and embody the spirit of the firm perhaps more than any other design. These objects with their distinctive sphere, an archetypical form that stands for perfection, remain an irresistible must-have due to their refined design and construction. In 2015 the large fragile Globe, the flat petite version and the gold-lustred variant of the series were all reissued.

Martino Gamper

### NEO 2016
„Passionswege" Vienna Design Week

„Ich wollte die Herausforderung annehmen, mit traditionellen Lobmeyr-Techniken neues und gegenwärtiges Ornament zu schaffen" – Martino Gamper ist bekannt für seine Neugier und seinen Sinn für radikales Experiment. Eine einfache Whiskeybecherform verwandelt sich durch Schleifen, Gravieren, Sandstrahlen, Malen, Vergolden und Lüstrieren in 54 unterschiedliche Gläser.

### NEO
*Passionswege* Vienna Design Week

"I wanted to take on the challenge of creating a contemporary ornament using the traditional Lobmeyr-techniques" – Martino Gamper is known for his curiosity and affinity for radical experimentation. A very simple whiskey tumbler form is transformed by cutting, engraving, polishing, sand-blasting, painting, gilding and burnishing into 54 different glasses.

Sebastian Menschhorn

### Blumenvasen BV71 – Kalebassen 2016

Schon in Urzeiten wurde der Kalebassenkürbis als Behälter verwendet. Die ungewöhnliche Form diente im Barock als Inspiration für Vasen aus Porzellan. Menschhorn spielt mit der Silhouette und verformt sie in mehreren Schritten. Drei sehr funktionale und spezielle Vasen in drei Farbtönen, Amethyst, Rosalin und Rauch-grau, sind das Ergebnis dieses Prozesses.

### Flower vases BV71 – Calabashes

The use of the calabash gourd as a vessel stretches back to primeval times. In the Baroque period its unusual form served as a source of inspiration for the design of porcelain vases. Menschhorn plays with the silhouette and warps it in several steps. The result of this process is three highly functional and special vases in three colors, amethyst, rosalin and grey.

Samuel Wilkinson

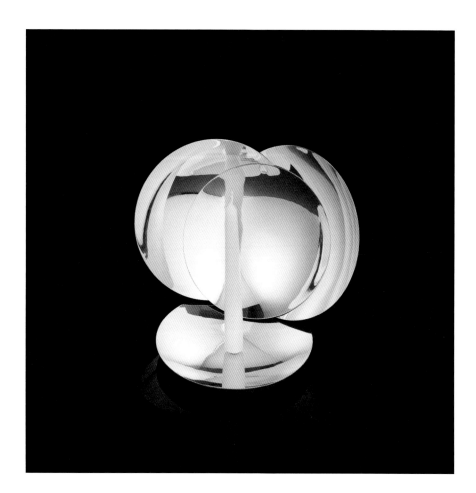

### Kerzenleuchter Zymbel 2017

Die Idee hinter der „Zymbel" war es, einen Kerzenleuchter zu schaffen, der den Schimmer einer einzigen
Kerze mit etwas Theatralik widerspiegeln und verstärken
würde. Die Form basiert auf vier sich verschiebenden
Scheiben, deren Aufbau sich innerhalb eines sphärischen
Raums nach Belieben ändern lässt. Die beschwerte Basis
ermöglicht es, dass die anderen drei Scheiben nach oben
und rund um die Kerze auskragen, sodass der Eindruck
entsteht, sie trotzten der Schwerkraft.

### Zymbel candle holder

The idea behind the *Zymbel* was to create a candle
holder that would reflect and amplify the glow from a
single candle with a bit of 'theatre'. The form is based on
four shifting discs, whose composition can be changed
as desired in a spherical space. The weighted base allows
the other three discs to cantilever up and around the
candle, producing a gravity defying appearance.

**6a architects**
2015
Desert Islands
Desert Islands
Wallpaper* Handmade 2015

**bkm – Stefan Moritsch**
2006
Undine
Undine

**Tomás Alonso**
2013
Pétanque – Wodka Set
Pétanque – Vodka set
Wallpaper* Handmade 2013

**Mark Braun**
2010
Trinkservice No. 283 – Reichtum
Drinking set no. 283 – Fortune
Vienna Design Week 2010
„Passionswege"

Seite Page 42–43

**Michael Anastassiades**
2012
Captured
Captured

Seite Page 52–53

**Mark Braun / Christoph Keller**
2013
Schnapsglas Stählemühle
Stählemühle schnapps glass

Seite Page 59

**Elliott Barnes**
2012
L'Alliance
L'Alliance

**Jack Canning for Alloy Yachts**
2013
Cunning Sphere
Cunning sphere

**BCXSY**
2014
Joy & Love Becher
Joy & Love tumblers
Vienna Design Week 2014
„Passionswege"

**Claesson-Koivisto-Rune**
2010
Vindobona
Vindobona
mit with Wiener Silber Manufactur

**David Collins**
2006
David Collins Luster
David Collins chandelier

Seite Page 29

**Thomas Feichtner**
2007
Axiome
Axiome

**Marco Dessí**
2009
Trinkservice No.281 – Grip
Drinking set no.281 – Grip

Seite Page 38 – 39

**Thomas Feichtner**
2011
one crystal chandelier
one crystal chandelier

**Marco Dessí**
2010
Basket Luster
Basket chandelier

Seite Page 46

**formafantasma**
2013
Trinkservice No.284 – Alphabet
Drinking set no.284 – Alphabet

Seite Page 58

**Marco Dessí**
2010
Trinkservice No.267 –
Alphablast
Drinking set no.267 –
Alphablast

**formafantasma**
2014
Serie STILL
STILL series

Seite Page 60 – 61

**Gregor Eichinger**
2010
Deep Space Becher
Tumbler Deep Space

**Martino Gamper**
2016
NEO – Whiskey Becher
NEO – Whiskey Tumbler
Vienna Design Week 2016
„Passionswege"

Seite Page 63

**Martino Gamper/
Kim Tien**
2006
Vienna Design Week 2006
„Passionswege"

**Sebastian Herkner**
2017
Taking Care
Taking Care
Wallpaper* Handmade 2017

**Oswald Haerdtl**
1925  2015
Kugeldose G und flach
G and Flat candy dishes

Seite Page 62

**Josef Hoffmann**
ca. 1930  2003
Hoffmann Ringvase
Limitiertes Jahresobjekt (180 Stück)
Hoffmann Ring Vase
Limited edition (180 pieces)

Seite Page 20

**Oswald Haerdtl**
1927  2015
Blumenvasen BV13
Flower vases BV13

**Josef Hoffmann**
1912  2015
Hoffmann A und B original
Hoffmann A and B original

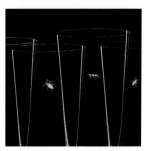

**Oswald Haerdtl
Murray Moss**
1954  2006
Trinkservice No.257 mit
Insektengravur
Drinking set no.257 with
insect engraving

Seite Page 28

**Josef Hoffmann**
1914  2014
Hoffmann Pokale
Hoffmann Goblets

**Oswald Haerdtl**
ca. 1950  2015
Stehlampe mit Faltenschirm
Floor lamp with pleated
lampshade

**Josef Hoffmann /
Michael Powolny**
1910  2003
Glockenvase
Bell shaped vase

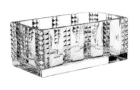

**Josef Hoffmann**
1912  2003
Prismenschliff Jardinière
Prism cut Jardinière

**KIM+HEEP**
2016
UFO – Hänge- und Tischlampen
UFO – Pendant and table lamps

**Lichterloh**
1952  2016
Trinkservice No.267 –
Normalzeit
Drinking set no.267 –
Normalzeit

**Florian Ladstätter**
2007
Orchideen Spiegel
Orchid mirrors

Seite Page 32 – 33

**Jack Ink**
2013
Venus Comb Shell
Venus comb shell

**Florian Ladstätter**
2007
Blockspiegel
Mirror block

**KIM+HEEP**
2012
Lily Tee
Lily Tee

**Max Lamb**
2009
Trinkservice No.267 –
Corn craft
Drinking set no.267 –
Corn craft

**KIM+HEEP**
2013
Lily Mokka
Lily Mokka

Seite Page 54

**Max Lamb**
2009
blowing-cutting-engraving
Vienna Design Week 2009
„Passionswege"

Seite Page 36

**Max Lamb**
2010
Quarz
Quarz

Seite Page 37

**LOBMEYR**
2010
Becher mit Spinnennetz und
Goldrand nach Biedermeieroriginal
Tumbler with spider's web and two
flies after Biedermeier-original

**Ernst Lichtblau**
ca.1930 2006
Tischlampe
Table lamp

**LOBMEYR for David Collins**
2008
Bellsize Park
Bellsize Park

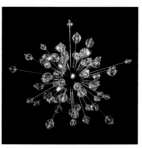

**LOBMEYR**
1930 2009
Minisputnik
Mini Sputnik

Seite Page 40

**LOBMEYR**
**Hans Harald Rath /**
**Leonid Rath**
1952 2004
Trinkservice No.267 – Alpha bunt
Drinking set no.267 – Alpha colours

Seite Page 21

**LOBMEYR**
1966 2005
MET Schmuck
MET jewellery

**LOBMEYR**
**Josef Lobmeyr**
1840 2007
Flakon No.8
Limitiertes Jahresobjekt (184 Stück)
Flakon No. 8
Limited edition (184 pieces)

Seite Page 34

**LOBMEYR**
2007
Trinkservice No.232 mit Fisch
nach Biedermeieroriginal
Drinking set no.232 with fish
after Biedermeier-original

**LOBMEYR**
**Johannes Rath**
2004
Becher Brand
Brand tumblers

**LOBMEYR**
**Leonid Rath**
2009
Blumenvase BV60
mit Chinoiserie
Flower Vase BV60
with chinoiserie

**LOBMEYR**
**Stefan Rath jun. /**
**Ernst Beranek**
2004
Megaron Spirale
Megaron Spirale

**LOBMEYR**
**Leonid Rath**
2009
Trinkservice No.267 –
Tulipmania
Drinking set no.267 –
Tulipmania

Seite Page 41

**Adolf Loos**
**Hubmann · Vass**
1931 2012
Loos Champagner Kühler
Loos champagne cooler

Seite Page 50 – 51

**LOBMEYR**
**Leonid Rath**
2009
Promenadenbecher
Promenade tumblers

**LucyD**
2005
RO Becher
RO Tumbler

**LOBMEYR**
**Louise Rath**
2009
Trinkservice No.257 Wasser-
becher mit Pinselstrich
Drinking set no.257
Tumbler with brush stroke

**LucyD**
2017
Wiener Melange
Wiener Melange
mit with Augarten

**LOBMEYR**
**Stefan Rath**
1955 2005
Blumenvasen BV60 bunt
Flower vases BV60 coloured

**Lucas Maassen**
2012
valerie_my_crystal_sister
valerie_my_crystal_sister
für for Vitra Design Museum

**Machytka & Schmoranz**
1877  2015
Krug No. 7887
aus der Arabischen Serie
Pitcher No. 7887
from the arabic series

**Sebastian Menschhorn**
2004
Serie Lebensblumen
Flowers of Life series

Seite Page 24

**MAK ART SOCIETY**
2012
MARS Collection
MARS Collection

Seite Page 49

**Sebastian Menschhorn**
2010
Serie Thom
Thom series

Seite Page 44

**Philipp Malouin**
2011
Time elapsed
Time elapsed
Vienna Design Week 2011
„Passionswege"

**Sebastian Menschhorn**
2013
Serie Eckhart
Eckhart series

Seite Page 55

**Miki Martinek**
1998  2005
Wiener Achtel
Wiener Achtel

Seite Page 25

**Sebastian Menschhorn**
2016
Blumenvasen BV71 –
Kalebassen
Flower vases BV71 –
Calabashes

Seite Page 64

**Sebastian Menschhorn**
2004
Serie Gletscher
Galcier series

Seite Page 22–23

**Sebastian Menschhorn**
Form Form
**Missoni, Westwood,
Cavalli**
Dekor Decoration
2013
Life Ball Champagner Kühler
Life Ball champagne cooler

**Sebastian Menschhorn**
2006
Kugelmonogramm
Pearl monogram

Seite Page 27

**Ted Muehling**
2010
Trinkservice No.282
Drinking set no.282

Seite Page 45

**Sebastian Menschhorn**
2004
Trinkservice No.267 mit
gemalten weißen Blättern
Drinking set no.267 with
white painted leaves

**Kostas Murkudis**
2009
Skulptur Chamaeleon für
Dysfashional
Sculpture Chamaeleon
for Dysfashional

**mischer'traxler**
2015
Installation Curiosity Cloud
Installation Curiosity Cloud
für for Perrier-Jouët at
V&A Museum

**Myung-Il-Song**
2014
Champagnerglas SONG
SONG champagne glass

**Murray Moss**
2017
Marylin
Marylin
für for Storefront for Architecture
and Design

**Peter Noever**
2005
MAK Achtel
MAK Achtel

**Ted Muehling**
2007
Trinkservice No.279 –
Balloon
Drinking set no.279 –
Balloon

Seite Page 30 – 31

**Gottfried Palatin**
2004
Vario Vasen
Vario Vases
mit with Augarten

**Dagobert Peche**
2016
Becher
Tumbler
für for Le Stanze del Vetro

**POLKA**
**Monica Singer/Marie Rahm**
2008
otto
Limitiertes Jahresobjekt (185 Stück)
otto
Limited edition (185 pieces)

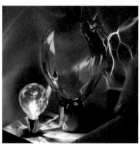

**poetic lab**
2013
Ripple Light
Ripple light

Seite Page 56–57

**POLKA**
**Monica Singer/Marie Rahm**

2008
otto
otto

**POLKA**
**Monica Singer**
2006
Josephine
Josephine

Seite Page 26

**POLKA**
**Monica Singer**
2007
Trinkservice No.267 – Ellipse
Drinking set no.267 – Ellipse

**POLKA**
**Monica Singer**
2011
Blumenvasen BV69 – drop
Flower vases BV69 – drop

**PRINZGAU/**
**podgorschek**
2010
Luster für Pfarre Tragwein
Chandelier for parish Tragwein

**POLKA**
**Monica Singer/Marie**
**Rahm**
2008
Trinkservice No.280 –
Wiener gemischter Satz
Drinking set no.280 –
Wiener gemischter Satz

**Talia Radford**
2015
CrystalJellies
CrystalJellies

**Robert Rüf**
2008
Vase Crinoline
Crinoline vase

**Tino Valentinitsch**
2011
Wiener Stutzen
Wiener Stutzen

Seite Page 48

**Sagmeister & Walsh**
2013
Trinkservice No.248 –
Sagmeister on Loos
Drinking set no.257 –
Sagmeister on Loos

Seite Page 47

**Maxim Velcovsky**
2008
City Shades
City shades
Vienna Design Week 2008
„Passionswege"

**Kay Sallier**
2014
Trinkservice No.267 – L.O.B.
Line of Beauty
Drinking set no.267 – L.O.B.
Line of Beauty

**Valentin Vodev**
2012
Piktogramme
Pictograms
Vienna Design Week 2012
„Passionswege"

**Kay Sallier /
Hubert Spoerri**
2016
Trinkservice No.267 –
Alpha – Ebenmaß
Drinking set no.267 –
Alpha – Ebenmaß

**Samuel Wilkinson**
2017
Kerzenleuchter Zymbel
Zymbel candle holder

Seite Page 65

**Oskar Strnad**
1925  2005
Kristalldose mit Chinoiserie
Crystal box with chinoiserie
Limitiertes Jahresobjekt (182 Stück)
Limited edition (182 pieces)

**Andrew Zuckermann**
2015
Trinkservice No.248 –
Birds on Loos
Drinking set no.248 –
Birds on Loos

Impressum                          Imprint

Herausgeber  Editors
J. & L. Lobmeyr (Leonid Rath, Andreas Rath, Johannes Rath)

Redaktion  Editing
Hubmann · Vass Architekten, Vienna

Autorin  Author
Kirsty Bell, London

Buchgestaltung  Book design
lenz+ büro für visuelle gestaltung
Gabriele Lenz und Elena Henrich, Vienna

Projektkoordination  Project management
Angelika Heller (Birkhäuser)

Lektorat  Proofreading
Angelika Heller, Monika Paff, Philipp Rissel (Deutsch)
Alun Brown (English)

Übersetzungen  Translations
Christian Rochow (ins Deutsche)
Joe O'Donnell (into English)

Herstellung  Production
Angelika Heller (Birkhäuser)
Elena Henrich (lenz+)

Bildbearbeitung  Image Editing
Verena Litzka (J. & L. Lobmeyr)

Schriften  Fonts
Corporate A / S (Kurt Weidemann, 1985 – 1989)

Papier  Paper
Arctic Volume White 150 g/m$^2$
Bindakote 250 g/m$^2$

Druck und Bindung  Printing and binding
Holzhausen Druck GmbH, Wolkersdorf

Library of Congress Cataloging-in-Publication data
A CIP catalog record for this book has been applied for
at the Library of Congress.

Bibliographic information published by the German
National Library The German National Library lists this
publication in the Deutsche Nationalbibliografie; detailed
bibliographic data are available on the Internet at
http://dnb.dnb.de.

This publication is also available as an e-book
(ISBN PDF 978-3-0356-1417-6).

© 2017 Birkhäuser Verlag GmbH, Basel
P.O. Box 44, 4009 Basel, Switzerland
Part of Walter de Gruyter GmbH, Berlin / Boston

Printed on acid-free paper produced from chlorine-free
pulp. TCF ∞
Printed in Austria

ISBN 978-3-0356-1407-7

9 8 7 6 5 4 3 2 1

www.birkhauser.com